MW00958374

2030 The Driverless World

- Business Transformation from autonomous vehicles

Stanford Edition

BY SUDHA JAMTHE

2030 The Driverless World

Published by Sudha Jamthe

Editor: Susanna Maier

Foreword: Brian Solis

Epilogue: Rob Van Kranenburg

Cover Design: Neha Jamthe

Image Credit: Sudha Jamthe

ISBN: 978-1973753674

Book Website: http://driverlesscarbook.com

First Published: Sep 2017 (Kindle Edition March 2017)

DEDICATION

To Mom

CONTENTS

Welcome to this Stanford Edition

Google self-driving cars returning to their base in Mountain View, California are my loyal companions each night as I drive back after teaching my Stanford CSP IoT course. They inspired my research to talk to the disruptors of autonomous vehicle space - leaders from the autonomous vehicle industry, automotive OEMs, transportation companies, regulators, global city leaders, venture capitalists. I reached a steady realization that the disruption is beyond Automotive and Transportation industries.

"Autonomous Vehicles are about the future of mobility."

We are witnessing a historic moment in mobility and the birth of new business models, new mobility designs, and the transformation of related industries—automotive, transportation, freight, insurance, infrastructure, retail, and others.

I had déjà vu recalling my eBay days in the mobile growth team where we built mobility solutions for the always-on customer.

The autonomous vehicle is going to create a mega-version of the always-on mobile customer with car data expanding the world of mobility services.

What services can an auto OEM offer customers if they know their intent and their behavioral patterns? What can new startups build to provide mobility services for parking, retail, infotainment, insurance or health services? How will this improve society locally and globally?

The autonomous vehicle is a business disruptor that is changing ownership patterns of vehicles. This is redefining the customer for automakers. This shift raises business model questions of whether the future will be a shared economy with ownership switching from consumers to a fleet. Will this commoditize the automakers and how are they going to deal with this disruption? Will creating a Blockchain ecosystem change the value chain?

The self-driving car will expand the Total available market (TAM) for mobility by bringing in new customer segments. Seniors, visually impaired or disabled users can become mobile with autonomous vehicles.

Can you imagine how a florist will change their retail space design when visually impaired customers show up at their store? How will theme parks change their business models if they know the intent of their potential customers who travel to their neighborhood using Autonomous Vehicle? The possibilities are endless spanning many industries that we don't associate with self-driving cars.

What about the future of autonomous car design? The

autonomous vehicle is going through a redesign to cater to the future mobile customer. Wheels, what wheels? Front facing? Why not make the car a round Pod? The options are limitless.

What business models will sustain and propel this innovation? Who are the winners and losers of the changing value chain? What is the role of Car Cognition technologies in shifting this space?

How will the city infrastructure scale to get ready for the autonomous world? Who is going to pay for this automation? In this transition to a driverless world, how will human driven cars share the roads with driverless cars?

Where are the gaps to innovate for entrepreneurs in all this? What industries are disrupted and how can corporate innovators manage this digital transformation? If you are looking for answers to these questions, this book is for you.

This research has led me to create a new course at Stanford Continuing Studies Program called "The Business of Self-Driving Cars" and this is the companion book for the class.

This course begins by teaching entrepreneurs and business leaders about the autonomous-vehicle landscape, covering everything from the technology of the self-driving car and Car AI to regulatory and policy issues and how to create value from autonomous-vehicle data. Each week we analyze industry players big and small. I have developed an Autonomous business framework for building new businesses in this dynamic space, and for creating new opportunities for companies. This framework will encompass mobility solutions, product management, design, market development, partnership, and business models. I guide my students, the innovators of tomorrow, to apply the business framework each week to build out their business plans. Students can optionally present their plans in teams to a panel of Autonomous Vehicle (AV) venture capitalists judges to understand the AV investment landscape.

I will not stop till I find the business drivers and explore business model evolutions and help entrepreneurs and corporate innovators shape the global autonomous vehicle ecosystem. I have updated the last kindle edition of this book into this Stanford edition with two new chapters one about business model evolutions and one about, Mobility Services. I have also shared the Autonomous Vehicles Business Framework with you in this book.

This book is for you as you set out to create innovations in new entrepreneurial businesses or existing businesses disrupted by mobility. Enjoy and be sure to share your experience with me.

- Sudha Jamthe, Technology Futurist, CEO IoTDisruptions.com & Stanford CSP Instructor, "The Business of Self-Driving Cars." @sujamthe, driverlessworldbook.com

Foreword by Brian Solis

Automotive 2.0: The New Road Ahead to Autonomous Vehicles

2021. That's the year auto manufacturers have promised fully autonomous vehicles on the road. This race is officially the latest tech gold rush. This date is also ambitious considering the sheer volume of technological, societal and also governmental challenges to solve between now and then. Initial applications for self-driving cars will be strewn across vertical applications, limited to fixed public transit courses, university and business campuses, warehouses, military applications, construction, farms and fields, and inner-city transportation services where infrastructure and pedestrian laws adapt for safety. Over time, applications will expand as technology advances, and prices come down.

Vehicles as Platforms – Opening up new revenue opportunities

Startups and technology leaders are driving the accelerated innovation in autonomous technology, forcing incumbents to partner, acquire, or ramp up R&D to compete (e.g. BMW and Baidu; Fiat Chrysler and Waymo, an Alphabet company; and GM and Lyft). Toyota, Intel, and Mercedes-Benz have dedicated business units. Automakers are getting into the software/hardware and utility business as future profits will depend less on manufacturing, selling and financing automobiles and more on monetizing driving and the free time passengers will have on their hands (instead of a steering wheel). Progressive automakers are repositioning their future to becoming mobility services and sharing companies. i.e. BMW, Daimler, Fiat-Chrysler, Ford, GM, Mercedes, Nissan, Tesla, VW, et al.

Cities must become smarter

While automakers are racing to 2021 for the release of autonomous vehicles, hurdles beyond technology are also tied to the lack of city infrastructure, modernization and policies.

As Automotive 2.0 creates new jobs along the way

Leading automakers are "acqui-hiring" startups through acquisition, partnership or investment to get talent in AI, machine learning, robotics, and deep learning to accelerate development. Since the entire idea of the car is evolving, the design of cockpits, services, and interiors overall are ripe for innovation. This will create a need for designers, UX/UI specialists, and architects to re-imagine passenger experiences.

Most consumers are not ready to give up driving

Driverless cars become machines rather than traditional representations of status, ownership, and pride. Many consumers believe that self-driving cars are inevitable but are content with driving. This leads to the next decade where human driven cars will co-exist with self-driving cars. This creates the need for the driverless car to learn the social communications of human drivers and pedestrians. Automakers such as Nissan and Audi are hiring anthropologists and social scientists to help build intelligent vehicles that can think and act more human.

Autonomous car makers are also becoming data companies

Every aspect of the vehicle and its environment is generating unprecedented levels of data. It's estimated that one car will use 4,000 GB of data per day. Machine learning, AI, deep learning, and data science overall, is needed to translate everything into value. This will lead to improved or new services, increased safety, new conveniences, better parking, greater fuel efficiency, faster delivery times, cheaper insurance, integrated payment systems, personalized experiences, and disruptive innovation. Carmakers will also become data companies, borrowing cues from Apple, Google, and Facebook to convert data into insights and customize consumer services to deliver value-added experiences.

Automotive 2.0: Redefining the Car for a New Generation of Services and Value

Automotive 2.0 completely changes the relationship between driver and automobile and manufacturer and consumer. No incumbent should assume that the brand can just shift gears to drive market performance. Automakers must create new value for customers. A vehicle becomes a blank canvas for new products and services and as such, creates a new paradigm for branding, monetization, and relationships. Automotive 2.0 sets the stage for vehicles-as-a-service to become differentiated products not by driver experience but instead by passenger accouterments. Additionally, manufacturers face the inevitable shift from the brand loyalty of today into more functional and lifestyle models where consumers employ automobiles-as-a-service.

Competitive value and differentiation will evolve from driver-centric features and existing cockpit designs to new and innovative spatial considerations and user experiences. We'll see car interiors that resemble lounges, offices, and living rooms. The very soul of automotive brands will now need to embrace new marque values, innovative technology, and experience design as part of its DNA.

With the autonomous industry racing from zero to warp speed, every aspect of the driving world is set for innovation and transformation. Whether you're navigating the self-driving world, affected by its progress, or shaping its future, it's essential that you rethink everything from brand to mobile services to value and every bit of infrastructure that supports getting from point b (before) to point a (autonomy).

This exciting and comprehensive new book by my dear friend Sudha Jamthe is your guide to understanding the future of self-driving vehicles and the new world to come. More importantly, her work helps us get smarter to accelerate our capacity to help share the future of the autonomous industry. In 12 sweeping chapters, you will become not only a self-driving expert but will clearly see the role you will play in bringing new autonomous business models to life and draw inspiration from her predictions of innovations all along the way until 2030.

Buckle up.

Brian Solis, digital analyst, anthropologist, futurist, a fellow passenger on the new roads ahead. @BrianSolis. BrianSolis.com

SUDHA JAMTHE

Praise for "2030 The Driverless World"

'AVs aren't just on the way, they're already here. Sudha takes us with her on a ride to the not so distant future of 2030 where auto AI is the new normal. Tapping her expertise in cognitive IoT, Sudha shares how driverless cars will communicate both with us and with our smart city infrastructure, providing the GPS for the transformation of passenger vehicles, semi trucks, and urban mobility.' - **Ken Herron CMO Unified Inbox Pte. Ltd.**

"The future Sudha Jamthe reveals in this book about cars as moral machines challenges our assumptions of what is a human-only domain as we create machines that learn their environment, respond to our emotions and reflect empathy. The future is now, and the legacy we leave for future generations is worth the careful consideration of our decisions made today." – **Tamara McCleary, Global Technology Influencer, and CEO, Thulium.co**

"Sudha takes us on a journey back from 2030, with a look into how the autonomous car is transforming industries and day-to-day life. It's fascinating to think that much of these predictions will no doubt be reality in the not-so-distant future." - **Zach Jory Digital Engagement Lead, IBM Watson IoT**

"If you are an aspiring entrepreneur looking to innovate in the autonomous vehicles space, this book is a must read". – **Natascha Thomson, CEO, MarketingXLerator**

SUDHA JAMTHE

CHAPTER 1: 2030 - A Cognitive IoT World

I have time traveled from the self-driving world of 2030. My world is a mix of autonomous vehicles and human driven cars with one in five being self-driving cars. Most self-driving cars are ride-share pods. The roads, traffic lights, parking spots, wearables on people, all communicate with the car seamlessly. They are connected, Cognitive Internet of Things (IoT). A Cognitive IoT is an ordinary thing with sensors that sends a large volume of data to the Internet and uses Artificial Intelligence (AI) to make sense of this data to solve problems with a speed that is unimaginable in 2017. For example, roads of 2030 are Cognitive IoT that use sensors to track road conditions, use AI to predict safety factors and communicate this to the car. So a road informs the car if it might skid or warn about a pothole after a storm in real-time, thereby improving the car safety.

In 2017, Traffic was a word humans could relate to with feelings of frustration. They were under the myth that they could control their commute times by speeding and caused accidents. Humans set out to build self-driving cars to avoid the 30,000 accidents caused by human error on American roads each year. Autonomous vehicles have improved road safety but have brought a much larger disruption of businesses, cities, and transportation by connecting everything and creating a two-way communication between humans and machines.

2017 is a special year in the disruption from self-driving cars. It was a time when cars were driven by all human drivers with an occasional self-driving car driving at a 25 mph limit with a human sitting inside. The city law required that the cars have a human driver ready to take over in case the self-driving car made any mistake. Unruly human drivers used to cut into bike lanes in the pretext of turning. Some pedestrians jaywalked onto the road in the middle of city roads, disrupting traffic flow. It was a time when it seemed impossible for a car's intelligence to decipher the many nuances of human communications. Humans used to blink their lights at other cars to let them go. Sometimes they honked at fellow cars to show annoyance and other times they honked to show support to a rallying crowd.

In 2017, driverless cars started sending messages to other cars which were known as Vehicle-to-Vehicle (V2V) communication. These were coded messages shared between the software running each car with data about the car's position, speed and what it was seeing at any given point in time. These helped autonomous cars predict what another autonomous car was going to do and adapt its driving for improved safety. But it did not help the driverless car communicate with the human-driven car or other things such as the road, traffic light and definitely not the pedestrian sharing the road. It was not yet evident that messaging was nowhere near enough for the self-driving car to fit into the social fabric of the road. This was a problem that limited the adoption of the driverless car from a human monitored 25 mph vehicle to drive autonomously with its full potential.

The next 10 to 15 years saw the transformation of businesses, cities, and disruption of human mobility in a fundamental way because the many communications of the car motivated us to build technology into everything to talk to the car. The car learned to communicate with its many stakeholders - the road, traffic lights, parking spots, wearables on humans inside and outside the car, the manufacturer, service dealers, other cars and more. The road would tell the car if it was icy; traffic lights and parking spots signaled the cars and the wearables on humans told the car about their health, emotions and their entertainment needs.

These transformative years saw many iterations of business innovations and business models and everything led to the development of Cognitive IoT. Mobility solutions switched from mobile phone platforms to the car. This drove the innovation and disruption of several industries, giving the opportunity for entrepreneurs and innovators to create new businesses, to find new uses of autonomous vehicles and to reimagine our transportation options. This propelled us forward to 2030.

So how did we get to 2030 from 2017? What are self-driving cars made of? How long do we have to go to a fully autonomous self-driving world? How did the car AI develop to speed up the many communications of the driverless car including the one with the human car driver sharing the roads? How did businesses manage this disruption? How did algorithmic governance of self-driving cars by Government regulations affect our lives?

As a technology futurist and author of three books about Internet of Things (IoT) focused on business disruption, my research led me to notice that IoT was creating large volumes of data bringing in Machine Learning, a part of AI technology. I could see the promise of Cognitive IoT, that made ordinary things smart with data predictions to solve new problems with amazing speeds. But IoT efforts were scattered across wearables, connected cities, smart home, connected cars and industrial IoT. There was no key driver that accelerated their pace.

Another factor I noticed in my work was about Social IoT, an area of Cognitive IoT where devices communicate with humans using voice and natural language processing. I saw Amazon Echo and Google Home begin to develop Conversational AI, a technology attempt to engage in continuous human conversation. Social IoT was also used in hospitals and cities using messaging between devices and multiple stakeholders. All of these were built upon Machine Learning, a technology that taught computers to develop patterns to make decisions using a large volume of data.

I got introduced to the working of a self-driving car from Sebastian Thrun and Katie Malone from their Machine Learning course on Udacity. It was fascinating to build out a classification algorithm that taught the car to make a decision to stop or go based on terrain type and slope. In 2016 Tesla introduced a video showing its self-driving, self-parking car showing what it saw using Computer vision. This got me curious about what a self-driving car really saw from its many sensors and how it made decisions from the software stored and running in the computer chip inside the car. I began observing and researching the many self-driving car pilots, most running in San Francisco roads.

As I drove back from my Stanford class at night, Google self-driving cars returning back to their base in Mountain View, California were my loyal companions. As much as I was fascinated by their constant speed and defensive driving among city drivers, it struck me how the car missed out on the social fabric of the road. As human drivers, when we saw a pedestrian standing in a divider, if we noticed that they were carrying a shopping bag, we empathized and signaled them to cross the road outside of pedestrian crossings.

The more I observed, I saw that there was constant human communication on the road. The self-driving car pilots were not communicating with each other or pedestrians and roads. I realized that we were in early stages of driverless cars and the real focus of self-driving car technology of 2017 was to develop its software AI brains to teach the car how to make safety decisions in unexpected situations related to other cars, pedestrians, or a child running into the road.

I realized how the driverless car has to make a transition, co-existing with human drivers, just like me watching the Google self-driving car. The car definitely had to learn multi-way communication to become a social machine among humans. Since this communication was going to be transmitted using technology, I could see clearly that every thing interacting with the car had to become a Cognitive IoT. **I determined that the driverless car would be the catalyst to accelerate Cognitive IoT not just in automobile but in industries all around it.** The cars cannot communicate with the road or traffic light or parking lot if they are not an intelligent, Cognitive IoT. As for the humans on the road and inside the car, I stipulated that it was going to be easy to communicate with wearables on the humans, rather than for the car to learn human language nuances. At CES 2017, I saw the early proof of this when Renault car company from France partnered with Sensoria Fitness of Seattle, where a driver would wear Sensoria powered shoes with sensors tracking their heart beat for safety at high speed bends to ensure it was within safety limits.

In this book, I share my analysis and predictions of these transformations from 2017 to 2030. The disruption will not stop with our personal cars. It will impact every industry it touches. It will change our cities. It will change urban mobility in new ways unimaginable in 2017. It will create new entrepreneurial opportunities as the car becomes the mobility platform of the future.

Join me as I tell you about **the technology and evolution of the car AI, walk you through how many Cognitive IoT devices developed symbiotically with the car's communication and guide you on how businesses made this transformation**. I will tell you about the transition we made as a society, as cities, and as global people to get to 2030. Together we will look at what lies ahead.

As you flip through the pages of this book, join me to step into a world of inspiration as we compare today with the autonomous driving world of 2030. We will look **at how our jobs, cities, and mobility of life are impacted by autonomous vehicles.** We will learn **how the nuances of human communication on the road was translated into technology by 2030, thereby creating many Cognitive IoT devices impacting cities, transportation and urban mobility.** We will look at **Industries disrupted** especially new Industries and business models in – Automotive, Transportation, Infrastructure, Cities, Farming, Freight, Ambulance, Recreation, Infrastructure, Hospitality, Retail, and Food industry. We will cover **business model evolutions and mobility services using Car data**. We will talk about regulation and governance **and how cities and countries adopted to the car's AI technology to ask for**

data and algorithmic governance of self-driving cars. A chapter will focus on what the self-driving car really sees to help us **understand the technology behind these autonomous vehicles.** Finally, join me to look ahead to how we can get to a fully autonomous driving world.

The audience for this book: This book is for you –

-   Stanford students from my IoT Business class who are an inspiration, ever curious to understand the Cognitive Internet of Things (IoT) ecosystem to stake their place in it with their promising business plans.

-   Entrepreneurs, Strategists, and Technologists from hardware and software background looking to fill in the gaps with innovative products and services.

-   If you are someone interested in how jobs will shift and what skills will be needed as self-driving cars scale mainstream.

-   Product Managers, Business Managers, Technology Strategists, Analysts, BPM specialists in Consumer and Industries space looking for ideas and inspiration on how Autonomous vehicles will transform their industries for – Automotive, Transportation, Infrastructure, Cities, Farming, Freight, Ambulance, Recreation, Medical, and Food industry.

This is not meant as a book for programmers looking for machine learning code and algorithms to build out self-driving car technology. Udacity has offered a great course for that since 2016.

CHAPTER 2: The Autonomous Vehicle Market of 2017

2.1 Market Size and Value Creation

I believe that autonomous vehicles create value by avoiding accidents by human drivers, saving fuel, and giving us peace of mind by reducing traffic.

Statista stated that the global revenue from self-driving cars is projected to be 42 billion dollars, with the US market estimated at 16 billion dollars by 2021. The autonomous car sensor market is projected to go from 417 million in 2015 to 26 billion dollars by 2030.

In 2017, Americans spent 7 billion hours commuting to work costing a total of 3 billion gallons of fuel or $160 billion. Cars were parked 95% of the time. 2017 was the year when people began to question the value of every person owning a car and about paying a monthly fee to cover the price of a car all their lives. Ride-sharing services such as Uber and Lyft were getting adoption. This was creating a new generation who chose not to learn to drive and were comfortable with not owning a car.

"California has 32 million actively registered vehicles putting 323 billion vehicle miles traveled per year," Bernard Soriano of the California DMV said at a talk at the Road Vehicle Automation Conference at Stanford in 2015. So, naturally, by 2017 twenty self-driving cars were given the first set of autonomous vehicle licenses and did test runs on California highways. Florida, Texas, and Arizona were also early adopter states to pilot self-driving vehicles in the US. London started testing driverless cars in 2015 and brought them to test drive on public roads in Jan 2017. John Deere piloted the driverless tractor in the farms of Germany beginning in 2008. Caterpillar launched 'CAT Command', the autonomous hauling vehicle that could respond to a shovel, haul to dump points, and report for maintenance.

2.2 Driverless Pilots of 2017

In 2017, consumer cars came in many forms such as sedans, hatchbacks, sports cars, rugged terrain Jeeps, SUVs, minivans for families, RVs for recreational long distance driving, race cars and much more. Their price varied widely dependent on consumers' brand sentiment of the automotive makers. These cars shared the road with commercial trucks and buses. The trucks included freight trucks, delivery trucks, construction trucks, mail trucks, ambulances and many specialty vehicles such as golf carts, limousines, moving trucks, and many more specialty vehicles.

By 2017, Google had spent 8 years in teaching the car to drive among humans and follow human road rules and behaviors. Their focus was on perfecting the autonomous vehicle technology. In 2015 the LUTZ driverless Pod created by RDM Group, UK, started testing in Milton Keyes. GATEway (Greenwich Automated Transport Environment) began testing a driverless shuttle testing in Greenwich, in UK with a mission to understand the technical, legal and societal challenges for driverless vehicle adoption in urban setting.

Image credit: GATEway shuttle from TRL, UK's Smart Mobility Lab

What was common among the self-driving cars and the John Deere tractors was that they had to have a human driver present, while the vehicle drove itself. Government regulation in both the US and Europe allowed for the driverless cars to be piloted in city roads but it required a human driver to be ready to take control in case the driverless car technology failed. The Google driver was a technologist who watched what the car saw and made it drive defensively and avoid accidents. The farmer on the John Deere tractor played with a mobile device while the tractor did precision farming in the fields of Germany.

The cars disengaged from driverless mode many times and gave control to the human driver. Each of these was called a 'disengagement' and the car companies had to file a 'disengagement report' to the DMV (American Department of Motor Vehicles) each year. The car technology was a black box so this was the government's way of understanding whether the car's algorithm was safe to continue driving among humans. Insurance companies were entering the foray supporting connected cars with sensors tracking driving patterns to gauge safe driver behavior.

Many Type of Autonomous Vehicle Pilots

Twenty automakers globally were testing self-driving cars and this number rose to 33 pilots in 2017 as many newcomers entered the scene. Some companies such as Google and Drive.io focused on creating the software for the driverless car. Others such as Zoox focused on creating the Cognitive software to create the car AI.

2017 is the year that it became obvious that the autonomous vehicle was becoming the next mobility device for the always-on consumer. Mobility was expected to shift from the phone to the car. Apple and Samsung entered the race in 2017 by getting California DMV permission to test self-driving car technology. Some bold efforts created unique autonomous vehicle designs which were drastically different from the cars of 2017. These were personal mobility vehicles that allowed an individual to ride a self-driving vehicle for urban mobility. Honda and Ford were the early innovators of this space.

Some shuttles tested out as autonomous vehicles. One called 'Loco' was tested in the Las Vegas strip. Another called 'Auro' ran as a college shuttle in Santa Clara University for campus mobility. These were simple self-driving vehicles with less complicated car software because they ran on a fixed route and machine learned to deal with disruptions along that short path from traffic lights and pedestrians.

Image Credit: Auro.ai AURO Self-driving shuttle.

Autonomous Vehicle Technology from Universities

Universities and corporations collaborated in enhancing the self-driving car technologies. MIT developed 'Nutonomy', a driverless car software technology. It tested this technology in self-driving taxis in Singapore and Dubai. Stanford tested an autonomous driving race car that it named as 'Shelley'.

University of Michigan's Transportation Research Institute, and University of Iowa, Florida International University all offered driving simulators. These helped with research at the junction of transportation and human factors. The driverless car needed to understand the human factors of communication of the human driver. So this became the foundation of the intelligence (AI) built into the cars we see on the road in 2030.

2.3 Boats Become Bridges

In 2017, bicycles, motorcycles and boats, began adding sensors to become connected IoT devices. These sensors allowed tracking of the vehicles to prevent theft. Some sensors tracked the air pollution levels as the bicycle drove along city roads. Amsterdam started with adding sensors to check for rising water levels to alert the owner when their boats started sinking in rising tides. By 2017 they successfully piloted 'Roboat', the autonomous boats of Netherlands led by a research collaboration between MIT's Senseable City Lab and AMS (the Amsterdam Institute for Advanced Metropolitan Solutions). These boats lined up and became bridges when needed and was the first step to test out water-based autonomous mobility solutions. These were all IoT devices but not yet intelligent to learn human communication. They began testing for 5 years from 2017 to solve for complex urban problems with water-based mobility solutions.

Image credit: MIT Senseable Lab and AMS (the Amsterdam Institute for Advanced Metropolitan Solutions) Collaboration Project.

These vehicles began learning from the driverless car as it was leading the way in becoming fully autonomous and in waking up consumers and city officials for compliance and regulation. Amsterdam traffic lights and bridges added sensors to communicate with bicycle riders. All these devices began machine learning, using the technology that allowed software to take data and make decisions with statistical models. They took all the data from driving pilots as input and produced an AI software that could make decisions about when to stop or accelerate the vehicle without human intervention. This allowed them to add intelligence to master their environments to become autonomous vehicles that could co-exist in the social fabric of society. They paved the way for the autonomous world of 2030.

In 2017, all focus was on building out the autonomous vehicle technology to make the cars drive safely without human support. Many companies were excited about the promise of a future, driverless world full of autonomous vehicles. They were not thinking about the transition period needed when the autonomous vehicle will share the road with the human driven cars. So they lost focus on how the autonomous car would communicate with the human driver and the many city infrastructures.

SUDHA JAMTHE

CHAPTER 3. Communications on the Road

Humans unconsciously abide by unwritten social rules on the road as drivers and pedestrians. These rules are riddled with human biases. In 2017, there was a field called Affective Computing where scientists were studying human-computer interfaces and how to teach machines to emulate emotions. But the autonomous vehicle makers were oblivious of the need for the many conversations of the driverless car.

3.1 Communication nuances

Conversation is not what we think of when we think of self-driving cars.

IoT Sensor Messaging is the beginning of the conversation with the driverless car and its many stakeholders. Sensoria Fitness, a

Seattle-based startup that makes wearables with the tagline, "The garment is the computer," is well on its way to do this with it's Renault car partnership where a driver wearing a Sensoria sock or shoes will have her pulse checked at high speed bends to check for safe limits. Davide Vigano, CEO of Sensorial Fitness postulates that the, "The driverless car could use such a wearable on a passenger to decide their alertness when it wants to transfer control in a disengagement scenario." In 2017, messaging, using data code between the car and an IoT device such as a wearable, was still a novelty. But over the next decade, we would realize that messaging of IoT devices from traffic lights and cars was not going to be enough to replicate human cognition of communications on the roads.

Car AI in conversations

Self-driving car pilots so far have been focused on building out computer vision, multiple sensors and radar hardware, and the deep learning software algorithms for the car to follow road rules and drive defensively reacting to other cars and objects crossing the road. In 2017, BMW and Ford were promising AI in cars in nearly 10 years. Such an AI would handle interactions of the human inside the car using an area of research called Affective Computing that teaches machines to emulate human emotions. With this, a car would know when the driver has road rage and could pull the driver over. Or on a more useful note, it could check if a passenger has gotten a heart attack and drive them to the nearest emergency clinic.

Is honking a conversation with a car?

Senator Gregg Harper asked Ford Motors at a US House subcommittee hearing on self-driving cars how a self-driving car would react to honking from another driver. Self-driving car makers did not have the answer for this in 2017.

Especially on the road, we humans have so many nuances in our communications. In 2017 it was impossible to imagine that an autonomous vehicle could learn this.

For the autonomous vehicle to interact with human drivers, the car AI has to learn the social nuances of our communications on the road. For example, I might honk when I see a friend at a traffic light or to show annoyance at someone cutting me on the road. Groups of drivers honk to show support to rallying crowds in America. How can a car interpret a honk as good or bad and decide the appropriate reaction? In 2017, the car would simply ignore the honking. Silence could not be the proxy for communication when the driverless car had to coexist with human drivers once it gets past the pilot stage.

WHAT DOES HONKING MEAN TO A DRIVERLESS CAR?
Annoyance? Get attention? Cheer?

Driverlesscarbook.com   #Driverless   @sujamthe | 10

Image credit Sudha Jamthe/A car passes by a rally on American roads.

Communication with Pedestrians

We would let a pedestrian cross not only at crosswalks but also out of kindness when we see a person standing with grocery bags at a divider in the middle of the road. The person should not have crossed the road half way in the first place but we might choose to stop for them to cross the road as we wait. Another driver may be irritated with jay-walking pedestrians and not like them waiting at the road dividers. As humans, our actions are full of our biases.

These biases made it complex by adding a morality question to our decisions about when road rules can be bent to accommodate rule-breaking behaviors of pedestrians or fellow human drivers on the roads.

Communication between drivers

In 2017, truck drivers and car drivers by bonded by the same road fatigue they felt on long highway drives. The truck drivers could spot hidden police cars waiting to catch speeding cars from their elevated seats and signal the car drivers to slow down. Car drivers would let other cars pass or merge onto a busy road by signaling them by flickering their lights. These were some of the many subtle communications between human drivers, which was beyond road rules.

NHTSA, the US Federal Highway Safety organization put forth a proposal that was reviewed in Q1 of 2017 that mandated vehicle-to-vehicle (V2V) communication on light vehicles, that allowed cars to talk to each other sharing information of their coordinates, speed, location etc. to avoid crashes. Some self-driving car companies opposed this saying this increased their liability exposure.

In Dec 2016, a Tesla Model S car driving under driver assist autopilot mode was able to predict an accident two cars ahead of a Tesla beyond the visible view of a driver and safely park the Tesla and saving a collision in Netherlands. It used Tesla Autopilot's Forward Collision Warning[5]. This added further proof for the need for autonomous vehicles to communicate with each other and share their coordinates to help each other navigate better to avoid collisions. The autonomous carmakers of 2017 were not focusing on these communications between a driverless car and a human driven car. They were not yet preparing for the transition years, where autonomous vehicles would co-exist with human driver cars.

3.2 Driver meets the Driverless Car

In 2017, drivers had a personal attachment to their car with a sense of ownership and control by driving their cars. Many drivers were unwilling to let the Car AI software drive it in the form of a driverless car. This created many segments of customers at different stages of adoption of a self-driving car, creating a challenge for Product Managers in defining what is the product of a self-driving car as this adoption cycle scaled over the next decade.

The technology evolution for the car to adapt to the social nuances was iterative and it made the road, traffic lights, parking spots, cars, bridges and the clothing on pedestrians and drivers into a cognitive IoT that built a tapestry of communication. This disrupted many industries over the next 15 years and got us to a new world of our co-existence with semi-autonomous and autonomous cars by 2030.

In 2017 we were talking about the self-driving car as if it was all about consumer cars freeing us from our daily work commute. The real disruption was on businesses – medical, freight, logistics, RV parks, construction, farming, moving companies, tourist companies, food, warehouses, airport shuttle services, city buses, hospitality, golf courses, delivery services and more. Except for a few, these businesses were oblivious to the disruption that was coming with the science fiction appeal of self-driving cars of 2017.

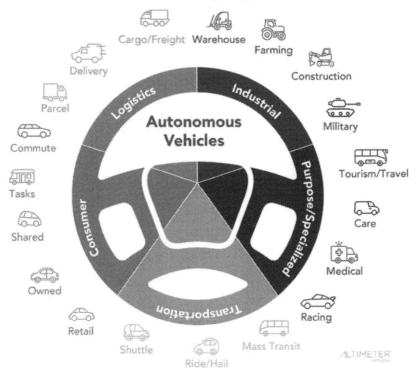

Image credit: Brian Solis. This picture shows the various applications of autonomous vehicles that spans over a wide range of industries.

But these businesses emerged as winners because they adopted the autonomous vehicle transformation beyond the innovation of the idea to the business value it offered. The business transformation created efficiencies for these businesses with on-time, safe deliveries and more consistency of experience to their customers which in turn increased business growth and revenues.

3.3 Services of Truck Drivers

Special trucks of all sizes covered a variety of uses in the transportation industry and came with a service person driving it. The mailman delivered paper mail. Firefighters saved people with fire trucks. Ambulances rushed people to hospitals in emergencies. In 2016, TU Delft University piloted an ambulance drone to create efficient ways to cut through the human driver car traffic to get to roadside emergencies quickly. That paved the way for ambulance drones remotely manned by emergency personnel. This made the ambulance truck driving on busy roads a rare thing by 2030. Golf carts and shuttles in the hospitality industry added to the hospitality of the business. A food truck driver was also the cook who served street food. School bus drivers made sure kids got in and out of the bus safely.

Tourist bus drivers were commentators inspiring tourists to visit important spots. City bus drivers were helpful navigators for passengers finding their way in a new neighborhood. The buses became smart to allow payments via biometrics with automated payments via BlockChain, sensing a commuter when they entered or left a bus. Construction vehicles were directed by humans with specialized skills, licensed to operate those vehicles safely and efficiently.

Every one of these specialty vehicles was tied to a human offering a service. So in 2017, it was hard to separate the cognition of the service person from the vehicle to even imagine it could become autonomous. Eventually, the specialty car drivers' role was separated as the driving part, their communications and the service they offered beyond driving. The driving was taken over by the Driverless car, and the communication was built into the technology of the car AI. The service layer of the driving human could not be replaced. These service jobs were enhanced to augment autonomous driving. This ended up saving the jobs of the many specialty vehicle drivers.

The last-mile of Commercial Trucks

Freight trucks carried food and supplies across cities. They moved our furniture cross-country. Freight logistics trucks with trailers carried parcels to deliver goods long distance. The drivers of tractors detached the big rig trailer body at warehouses to swap supplies. The trucks contributed to 7% of the traffic congestion but bore $28 Billion (28%) of the congestion cost for fuels, bringing down the efficiency of truck businesses.

In 2017 there were 500,000 trucking companies in America moving goods to retail, banks and even our water supplies. Trucks have elaborate processes to follow at their delivery destinations which made the role of the driver critical in the last mile of the drive. The truck driver handed over the products they delivered to the warehouse or retail store or hospital or gas station. So the autonomous trucks drove with a human driver who rested during the drive but took care of the last mile to communicate with the warehouse or the delivery agents at its destination. Every one of these truck drivers played a key role in the complex process of interacting with the business at the receiving end to ensure delivery satisfaction and service level guarantees. Similar to the specialty vehicle drivers, the truck drivers' jobs were enhanced to handle the last-mile service level guarantee of their businesses and were saved.

The communication on the road between the human driver and pedestrians was nuanced and riddled with biases making it difficult for the car AI to learn it. The specialty trucks and freight truck drivers added value to their customers with their communication, offering a service layer, which was not obvious until the autonomous vehicles showed that human communication cognition on the road was not easy to replicate using AI.

This led to two important changes. First, the autonomous vehicles ended up automating only the driving part of their jobs and the drivers retained their communication service part of their jobs. Second, wearables became a proxy for the human driver's and pedestrian's communication intents and paved the way for the creation of Cognitive IoT systems that facilitated interaction between the driverless cars and the human driver driven cars.

SUDHA JAMTHE

CHAPTER 4 Technology: What a Driverless car sees

As human drivers, we see the whole road including several cars, buses, the road with many lanes, some wetness and dirt on the road, the traffic signs, and pedestrians walking. In all this, we don't miss the blue sky and the rainbow we sometimes see amidst the traffic, which helps put a smile on our face as we ride on. I wonder what is a self-driving car seeing and how?

What does 'driving' mean for a self-driving car?

Driving for a self-driving car means making decisions every step of the way about the angle of the steering wheel and whether to stop or pick up speed and when to change lanes or take exits. The car has to identify lanes on the road, identify various objects such as traffic lights, speed signs, crossing pedestrians and other cars on the road. It has to predict what other cars and people on the road are going to do based on their current movement. The car has to constantly make sense of all these inputs and make decisions to move or stop. As a computer, it has to store all this data and send it to the cloud to the manufacturer for a health check about its driving.

4.1 Self-Driving Car Hardware

A human driven car is a mechanical device that keeps the car accelerating or stops based on the driver's action. The human driver watches the road for others, looks for traffic signs, sudden construction signs, and for any random pedestrian crossing their path. They are aware of road rules of when to stop and when they have the right of way but still are on the alert for other cars that may not follow road rules and may end up in a collision. The human driven car sees directly through the front windshield and uses mirrors for side-view and rear view. The driver seamlessly processes all the activities on the road and keeps driving or makes decision to stop or turn.

The driverless car has the mechanical framework of the regular human driven car. The car has a brain that has the AI that has learned road rules and how to make decisions. It has a lot of sensing hardware and cameras to compensate for the human driver's vision to capture all objects and activities of the road.

A human driver watches the road in all directions naturally with her eyes. The car develops computer vision using an input from a variety of sources that watch the road all around it. These are proximity sensors, radar sensors, laser sensors using Lidar, and video cameras. The car collects the same information using multiple sensors to triangulate and get an accurate picture of objects such as other cars, people, road conditions, lanes, traffic lights and any surprise object that may show up on the road.

LIDAR: The Driverless car typically have a laser sensor device such as a Velodyne 64-beam laser, that keeps rotating and collecting 360 degree information around the car. It makes a 3D model of what is around the car and the distance from the car.

Radar: Radars on the front, back and sides of the car help it gather information about the distance of other objects around it and how fast they are moving.

Cameras: The cameras capture videos that show the lanes as multiple image frames to help the car with lane detection, traffic sign and traffic light detection. The videos also help the car use computer vision to figure out the distance of nearby objects and uses this information to determine the direction of other moving objects on the road.

Sensors: Proximity sensors collect data about objects static and mobile on the lateral sides of the car.

GPS: Used for location the vehicle's location and trip planning.

4.2 Machine and Deep Learning Software

The brain behind the autonomous car software is a set of algorithms built using Machine Learning and Deep Learning technologies. Machine Learning is the technology by which the computer takes lots of data and uses computer models to develop the software that makes predictions and decisions.

Lane Detector – This is a software module that helps the car identify lanes on the road. In lane detection, the computer identifies where are the lanes on the road at any given second. The car uses this information to stay within the lanes. Lane detection is a hard problem to build models for different road conditions of bright sunlight, rain or snow, for different type of lanes, lane shadows or missing lanes. It gets tricky when the road curves and there are other objects such as dividers and walls on the edge of the roads.

In early stages of development of lane detection technology, it was done using Computer Vision, a technology that helped computers collect, interpret and make decisions of frames of images or videos. Deep Learning has replaced this by feeding videos of several real roads to the self-driving car to teach itself about lane detection with a high degree of accuracy.

Curvature = 1241.0m
Vehicle is 0.12m left of center

Image Credit: Shirish Jamthe's open source Computer Vision lane detection model. This picture shows what a self-driving car sees as the lane and the curvature of the road. It uses this to decide how much to turn its steering wheels to stay within the lane.

Using the lanes detected, the car makes constant calculations of how much to turn the steering wheel to stay within its lane as it keeps moving.

Objection Detection – Traffic signs, Road signs & Obstacles

The autonomous vehicle learns to identify traffic signs using Image recognition and Object identification, both use machine learning technology. A computer model is trained on a large computer with a powerful GPU on the cloud, with thousands of images of road signs in all conditions of wear and tear, light conditions and viewing angles as training data. Next it is trained on Object identification to read posted road speeds and other words on the road signs. These create the models that are stored on the car's software. These models help the car identify road signs and what they mean. When the car sees an object on the road, its software uses the models it has onboard to run a prediction to decide if it is a traffic sign or a road sign that it has learned about or is it an obstacle. This predictive module of the car is the Object detection module software.

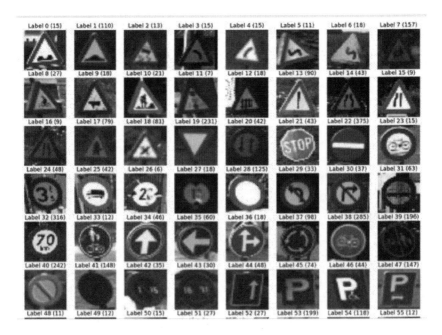

Image Credit: Waleed Abdulla's open source traffic sign recognition software model. This shows how the car sees the different traffic sign images to learn to identify road signs.

This same object detection technology is used to identify other objects on the road. Another car or a pedestrian are both treated as objects by the Driverless car. It uses Deep Learning to teach the car to identify objects on the road. Deep Learning is an advanced technology, next step to Machine Learning where the computer takes lots of training data, and figures out what the different objects and patterns are without any personal guiding what signals the computer should look for in the data. This removes the limitation of what signals a human might expect the computer to learn in the training data. For example, when a person sees a scene they observe many things and recall different objects as being similar to other objects that may have seen in their lives. This is how the human brain identifies things even when presented in various context. For example, instead of learning that a traffic sign for 70 miles speed is what it is in an image, humans learn numbers and identify 7 and 0 anywhere they see as 70. They learn traffic signs as being a particular shape and size and expect to see them in certain parts of the road at a certain height. So when they see the traffic speed limit sign, they identify it naturally without any ambiguity. Neural networks allow the computer using deep learning to learn an environment similarly. This is applied to object detection in driverless car technology to let the car identify the signs independent of their angle, wear and tear and any weather damage to the sign, naturally with a close to a human-like cognition of objects.

Image Credit: Shirish Jamthe's open source Deep Learning neural network model identifying vehicles. This is how the self-driving car will see other cars.

Predicting other cars and people

The autonomous cars have a prediction algorithm that uses all the information about the objects in the road and their speed and positions to predict their actions. Tesla cars have developed what they call as fleet's learning ability. Tesla collects data from its fleet of cars running even driven by drivers crossing a GPS location to create a map of the driving world and make note of driver behavior of when they brake at certain locations. It applies machine learning and uses this information as training data to create models to be used by future Tesla cars. They use this model with real time road conditions and objects to make predictions about the movement of other cars on the road. The Tesla in autopilot mode will apply a mild brake even if their optical cameras do not see an obstruction based on the knowledge gathered from their fleet's learning ability model.

Tesla Model S and Model X have 10,000 cars with radars that drivers switch to autopilot, their autonomous driving mode. These cars send millions of GB of data to Tesla cloud daily. Tesla uses this as training data to fine tune their autonomous vehicle software technology. Tesla develops predictive algorithms that the car can use to watch for behaviors of other cars on the road. A Tesla used predicted the accident of a car, two cars ahead of a Tesla and took immediate action and saved the Tesla car and driver. It is important to note that this learning is not happening in not real time in the car. The car software company keeps learning from many new car driving scenarios to improve their models. But it is important to note, that the car does not have the latest model until it receives it as a software update from the company. This is where the next model, OTA comes in.

OTA (Over the Air) Software Updates

Self-driving car companies keep updating the software in the car and keep sending updates over the air wirelessly similar to OS upgrades we get on our computers. This sends patches for quick fixes and ongoing updates to keep their software AI sharing its learning without any disturbance to the driver. This way cars become better even after you bought them from the dealer.

Diversions: Construction

Construction areas are a challenge for driverless cars. What might look like a standard construction zone to a human driver is a surprise condition that the autonomous car has trouble identifying what is going on and to make decisions on how to navigate the signs for lane closures and mergers. So, the car software is on the constant lookout for any interruption from unexpected objects and events.

Algorithm to make driving decisions

The car has a real-time operating system, which it uses to apply the models it had learned and make decisions to accelerate, stop or turn at every point in the road. It is a continuous decision it makes that keeps the car moving on the road. Though it might seem like a simple software that the car will machine learn, this is where any boundary conditions of how the car will make moral decisions in rare situations where it has to decide to stop or proceed between two risky situations that might kill a human. We will talk about this moral dilemma later in the book. Today, there is no transparency on what these boundary conditions are and how the driverless car software his programmed for the available autonomous vehicle pilots on the road.

Event Data Recording

The car stores data from its various sensors and its location and data about the decision it makes for every second in time. This data is reviewed by the engineers after each drive during the self-driving car pilot to get insights on whether the car makes decisions as expected or if there is any bug in its software that needs fixing. This data is similar to a flight black box data of a plane and gives clues about how the car made decisions and where it needs further training. This information is also used to create drive simulation so future software can be tested before it is pushed to the cars.

V2V communication

In 2017, the US government mandated driverless car companies to share their data to help each other be aware of the intents of other driverless cars. This is called V2V communication. V2V was a new concept in 2017, with no standards on what this data was going to be. Companies were getting ready to share the minimum data mandated by the government. I believe that they are planning on building their own predictive algorithms to give them a competitive edge in developing the best self-driving car. In 2017, there was no technology being planned about sharing data between driver driven cars and driverless cars.

Software Simulation Package

A simulation package is a software for the self-driving car to recreate the conditions and decisions made by the car when there was any problem such as a crash or a disengagement from autonomous mode by the human driver piloting the car. This simulation software pioneered by Google is a critical part of the learning development of a self-driving car required by all self-driving car software makers.

Disengagement self-check modules

These are pieces of software baked into the brains of a self-driving car that always checks itself to see if there was any risk condition that it needs to disengage from self-drive mode during the phase when self-driving cars still had a standard driver ready to take control. This served as an alert module for the car to self-check if it hits any boundaries of its autonomous learning capabilities to avoid crashes. In March 2017, Uber shocked the world with its disengagement report that showed that the self-driving car was taken over by the human driver every mile on an average. Each of these was an opportunity for Uber to improve the self-driving car software.

Open Source Driverless Technology

Udacity was a pioneer in creating the first open source car by teaching the first online driverless car software class. Udacity engaged a global community by posting competitions to develop the best machine learning car models. It posted it all in open source with the aspiration to build out an open source driverless car for the world to use.

Image Credit: Sudha Jamthe. Picture shows tweet by Oliver Cameron, then VP Engineering and Product at Udacity (now CEO of Voyage) showing what a self-driving car sees as lanes on the road.

MIT followed with a Deep Learning for Self-Driving Cars: 6.S094 but did not put the models in open source. MIT took 10 Tesla cars and offered the course online for free for the world of developers to build models and submit their code and data to test on the Tesla cars. These were pioneers that brought the self-driving car technology to global developers and nurtured the aspiration of an open source car possible. Comma.ai developed a limited version of open source hardware and software add-ons that would make limited car models into a Driverless car. These set the foundation to create transparency of what was under the hood of a self-driving car setting the promise for a world of developers to collaborate and develop open standards.

4.3 What we learned from the Pilots

2017 was the year that accelerated the self-driving car pilots and taught valuable lessons in the machine learning software technology of the driverless car. Every crash or disengagement of the car was a problem exposed that the car AI learned to avoid when it rolled out of the pilots in the next five years.

The typical way a software programmer writes code is to write it for various scenarios and test it and see where it fails. Failure is a good thing because it shows the bugs in the code. They iterate and make improvements to make a better product. Silicon Valley's way of iterate and test is based on giving a Minimum Viable product (MVP) to customers, call it beta and look for bugs to fix. Self-driving vehicles are built using Machine Learning, which runs on training data, teaching the car about various scenarios. So the iterate and test model end up with crashes, and it informs and improves the code. The problem with self-driving car software code is that the trial is in real road conditions with humans and other cars and each crash put life and property at risk. So each crash of a self-driving car pilot gets scrutinized.

So in 2017 cities asked for disengagement reports to help them understand the real state of readiness of the autonomous vehicles to improve the regulation process better. It is important to remember that car makers tested these cars in simulation environments and test tracks before they applied for an autonomous vehicle license to run pilots on city roads and highways. But in 2017, there was no benchmark on what was the minimum safety requirement for an autonomous vehicle technology quality before it applied for a license. At least there was no transparency or standard for this level of technology globally for self-driving car pilots.

Crashes are unfortunate, but each disengagement of self-driving car pilots taught us something each time and helped the industry propel forward. Sometimes these disengagements were done voluntarily by the car driver when the car data showed different data than what the company expected it for decision making which had a potential to cause a crash.

The following is the top set of reported self-driving car pilot results and what improvements they propelled in the driverless car technology of 2017.

1. **MIT's Nutonomy self-driving car technology** – MIT piloted this in Singapore Taxis between two fixed points, and it ended with a crash. MIT fixed it and resumed the pilot.

2. **Tesla's Autopilot** Crash – Tesla added auto-pilot mode in its current cars and said the driver could turn it on and bear the risk if they do not watch the road and take over the car out of auto pilot mode. In 2016, a Tesla driver died letting the car run in the highway in Auto mode while being negligent, watching a movie. Tesla was absolved any blame for the crash. But what caused the car to continue to plow into a truck in Auto mode is shocking. George Hotz of Comma.ai said that Tesla Autonomous Software could not differentiate between a moving and a fixed object. So when the car came to a crossing and saw a huge truck crossing it, it thought that it was a bridge and attempted to go under it and plowed into it. Tesla used this crash to

develop a very unique technology to improve its car AI. It started to collect driver behavior at various geographic locations and used this as additional information for the car to make decisions at any point on the road. So when the car AI sees a bridge and expects to plow through it, but the aggregate data of other drivers shows them stopping and letting the presumed bridge move, then the car gets smarter to learn that it was a truck and not a bridge.

3. **Uber's ATX Pilot in Philadelphia** – Uber was caught going on the other side of the road and quickly reversed by the driver to go the right side. Uber must have improved its lane detection to make sure the car does not enter the wrong side of the road.

4. **Uber's Pilot in San Francisco in Dec 2016** – Uber staged a standoff with the city of San Francisco claiming it didn't need an Autonomous vehicle license from the city. The car jumped a red light, and Uber claimed it was the fault of the human driver who didn't stop it and fired the person. The self-driving car technology apparently was not developed enough to know traffic lights, which was a critically limited system not ready for the roads. So San Francisco state attorney general issued a cease and desist and stopped the Uber pilot. Uber in this case needed to add a lot of training data for the car to learn object identification to stop at traffic lights.

5. **Otto's Autonomous Truck Pilot** - Otto did a 127-mile ride on Michigan roads in Oct 2016. It was uneventful and was the first for a Truck to drive autonomously. By March 2017, Otto's technology is disputed by Google raising the question that they had Google's self-driving car software with its eight years of machine learning experience.

6. **Truck Platoons** - Truck Platoons is an autonomous driving technology whereby many trucks followed one truck and drove autonomously together on the highway. This was piloted as the EU Trucks Platooning Challenge on European highways by six car brands covering five countries and 2000 km successfully. This proved that we could save fuel by platooning trucks as they reduce the drag and consume less energy. It also demonstrated the use case for using autonomous trucks for infrastructure and mining in industrial businesses.

7. **Stanford's race car "Shelly"** - This was a race car pilot that tested an autonomous vehicle as a race car. It helped design better race cars.

8. **Loco pilot in Las Vegas** - This was a pilot where the shuttle ran on a fixed route as an autonomous vehicle driving

passengers from the Las Vegas Strip to the airport.

9. **LUTZ Pod in Milton Keynes** - This was a test pilot that helped develop many iterations of self-driving cars in UK.

10. **GATEway Shuttle in London** - This was a pilot similar to the Loco in Las Vegas, US and proved the safety of making autonomous vehicle technology for fixed routes. GATEway's goal was to study the consumer adoption to learn the legal and social implication of the various use cases of an autonomous vehicles.

11. **Uber SUV flipped in accident on Arizona** – On 30th March 2017, a self-driving Uber SUV was hit by a human driven car. It flipped the Uber onto its sides. It turned out that the human driver did not yield to the Uber, which had the right of way. This taught the Uber to not assume humans will follow all road rules and to drive more defensively.

All these tests of 2017 fed training data for the machine learning algorithms and helped improve the car software to run confidently. The MIT Nutonomy pilot in Singapore taxis, LUTZ in Milton Keyes and Loco in Las Vegas all proved that a basic level autonomous vehicle could be deployed successfully without teaching the same vehicle the complex rules of city driving. This laid the foundation for future machine learning technology that developed with the Car AI into the autonomous vehicle technology of 2030.

These pilots also helped the driverless technology makers to decide which road conditions were safer to launch the initial set of driverless cars. This led to automaker (OEMs) incorporating some autonomous features into existing human driven cars to get people comfortable with some basic autonomous features. The eventually led to shuttles and taxis inside colleges, airports, golf-carts, and some industrial areas on fixed path roads. These were basic Level 1 or Level 2 autonomous vehicles that become the early self-driving vehicles to reach mass market.

CHAPTER 5 Transformation of Industries

The Driverless car is going to share the road with the human driven car for a transition period of more than 10 to 15 years. This is a time of transformation for several industries. Automakers have been introducing new designs for the autonomous vehicle. They are debating whether we need a steering wheel in a fully autonomous vehicle. There are new categories of vehicles being introduced. This is disrupting many industries with Automotive and Transportation industries being the most impacted. The efficiency of driverless cars is going to impact many other industries that use any form of mobility vehicles such as medical ambulances, school buses, shuttles, golf carts, delivery trucks and much more. City infrastructure is going to adapt to the need to communicate with the car. This combined with a huge volume of city data will accelerate the city becoming a Cognitive IoT.

5.1 Automotive

The automotive industry makes cars, commercial vehicles, car parts and runs dealerships to sell cars. They produced 68.56 million cars and 22.12 million commercial vehicles globally with only 1.3 million of these being electric cars by 2016. The automotive industry was at a cusp of disruption with autonomous vehicles in 2017. Google, Volkswagen, Nissan, Delphi, Bosch, and Mercedes-Benz have tested autonomous vehicles on public roads by end 2016 with Google (Waymo) ahead of the pack with 1.4Mil tested miles. Tesla was disrupting the autonomous vehicle's market by launching its autopilot mode in conventional cars, which offers lane assistance on highways and shared a video showing a more advanced self-driving, self-parking car feature in its Model 5. Tesla had produced 100,000 cars in four years of its life, but within days it had a pre-order booking for 400,000 Tesla Model S, which it had promised to start shipping out by early 2017.

Most major Auto brands have promised 2021 as the year they will launch a self-driving car with varying levels of automation.

The global revenue from self-driving cars is projected to be 42 billion dollars with the US market estimated at 16 billion dollars in 2021. The autonomous car sensor market is expected to go from 417 million in 2015 to 26 billion dollars by 2030.

All paths lead to 2030

In 2017, while the cars were still being piloted with a human driver ready to take control, different automakers perceived customer acceptance of fully autonomous cars differently. This lead to a wide variety of car designs for driverless cars. Some automakers wanted to design the autonomous car with a fresh look and not as a translation of the current human driven cars. So they wanted to remove the steering wheel altogether. Ford and Honda created a whole new class of vehicles for personal mobility that did not resemble the car of 2017 in any way. The decade following 2017 saw a lot of iteration of new car designs and new ways to solve the mobility problem for the consumer. The commercial vehicles industry, on the other hand, focused more on safety and uninterrupted service over design.

Customer and Brand Shifts

The more subtle shift in the automobile industry was in how they adapted the transformation of what value the car offered to consumers. In 2017, consumer cars come in many sizes, shapes, colors and features to cater to various customer segments. There was a camp of innovators who believed that they could retrofit the self-driving car technology into the cars of 2017 and make them autonomous driving cars. So a Volvo would become a self-driving Volvo, and a Subaru will become a self-driving Subaru. But as the driverless cars were introduced, customers will evolve with new needs. It was inconceivable to imagine a personal mobility robotic vehicle for personal use in 2017.

Let us look at the Driverless car as a new product. The core technology to teach the car to drive in road conditions safely is the same. Beyond that, each car has different product features it offers and has built its brand out on that. BMW is known as the ultimate driving machine with Tesla challenging it by early 2017. Volvo is sold as a safe car. A Subaru is a rugged terrain car for the backpacker.

The first change automakers had to adopt was to rethink of their cars not as mechanical machines but electro-mechanical machines controlled by intelligent software. Many Automakers opened innovation centers in Silicon Valley to partner, develop the skills needed and build the competencies to partner with software players to embed the self-driving car technology into their vehicles. Meanwhile, similar innovations happened in China and Europe. So the Subaru demanded more modules that made sure the self-driving car could run in mountainous terrains and cater to its customer base.

Next, they had to re-think their brands. Tesla cut into BMW's market as the Ultimate driving machine with soaring demands and selling pre-orders of $1Billion for its Model 3 within days. BMW responded by sharing its 2020 manifesto showing an AI in the car guiding the driver. Toyota introduced its 2030 Concept car. The real issue was how customer usage of the cars was changing, and the customers were looking at the cars as a different product, not as the same brand from before.

New uses of the cars evolved as self-driving cars became more mainstream. Ride sharing was one business model everyone could see because of the growth of Uber, Lyft, Didi Chuxing of China. So if a company bought cars and used it for ridesharing, it was a different market, a B2B market instead of a direct to consumer market. So dealership networks had to adapt to this massive business disruption first. Consumers who would lease vehicles were now expected to lease a self-driving car from the dealers. The dealers who once sold leases saying it was a deal to lease a new car every two years instead of buying and paying the car mortgage and maintenance fees were stumped.

The self-driving car was a different product. It tracked its maintenance needs and drove itself for service proactively. IoT technology sensors were added in all car accessories. Michelin tires added sensors to check for tire pressure proactively and predict and avoid flat tires. All these contributed to consumers distancing themselves from the car maintenance pain, which was soon forgotten. Then the dealers adapted to the new customer usage of automobiles. They changed to cars sold to offices to become traveling team pods. Consumers rented cars on-demand based on their travel plans for tourism or vacation. As the cars came with different capabilities, the dealers adapted and understood the evolving customer segments and became successful.

The open question remained on what do consumers want? How to segment them to offer different cars that help everyone and keeps the growth of automotive industry.

5.2 Connected Transportation

Image Credit: Venture Scanner map of the evolving Transportation industry.

In 2017 cars were owned or leased by consumers or rented from rental companies. Ride sharing had just begun a few years back. Trucks were owned by truck companies and did delivery of all essential and industrial items. Before autonomous vehicles, trucking was a fleet business. Once the trucks became connected with sensors and Internet connectivity, trucking as an industry went through a huge disruption. On one end there was the speculation of trucker's jobs being replaced by autonomous vehicles, and on the other end, there was the promise of trucking industry going through a business transformation to become a part of a new connected Transportation industry.

Delivery trucks and shuttles were the first ones to continue on their existing business models. Delivery trucks and shuttles drive along known routes so they could be geo-fenced and tracked for accurate, safe driving without the complexity of the consumer car driving city roads.

Platooning Trucks

As transportation companies adopted the reality of autonomous vehicles, they tested out platooning trucks focused on fuel efficiencies and reducing emissions. Platooning is the method by which several trucks follow each other in a row with the first truck driving the whole platoon. This creates energy efficiency and reduces accidents with the trucks communicating autonomously with each other and stopping or moving in unison.

Drive Assistive Truck Platooning (DATP) is the technology that allows a driver at the front to control a platoon of trucks. By 2017 DATP technology was developing satisfactorily to make truck platooning a reality by 2030. By 2017 the real challenge to truck platooning was the strict regulation on trucks to keep the safety of cars sharing the road with trucks. These regulations were being reviewed by the various US state to adapt to make truck platooning a reality. Volvo Trucks were fitted with Peloton DATP technology. They did a successful test-run in Berkeley In partnership with PATH (Partnership for Advanced Transportation Technology of Berkeley) in March 2017. This paved the way for scaling Truck Platooning in the US.

The European Trucking Platooning Challenge piloted platooning across Europe for several years. In early 2017, Germany demonstrated a three-truck platoon with Daimler Trucks. This proved the viability of connected trucks platoons sharing the road with cars. The UK decided to start the first Platooning truck project in 2018 making this a mainstream disruption for the trucking industry. Meanwhile, Scania, the Trucking company who participated in the European Platooning Challenge decided to start full scale autonomous platooning operations in Singapore in 2017.

Multi-user vehicles market transformation

Automobile manufacturers started building in sensors and multi-seater vehicles for ride sharing. The multi-user vehicles such as vans, shuttles, and delivery vehicles went through similar changes. They realized that they could not survive in a transforming industry by just adding self-driving software modules and computer vision LIDARs to their vehicles. They realized their expertise was in building out the mechanics of the car catering to their customer needs and that was shifting, but the need was greater than ever.

So they honed into their customer needs and rebuilt their vehicles with necessary sensors and mechanics. For example, delivery trucks were retrofitted with refrigeration with sensors ensuring the products were maintained at the required temperatures.

Ambulance trucks were retrofitted with telepresence and remote diagnostics capabilities so the emergency personnel could save lives while in the vehicles by sharing the patient's vitals and doctors could deliver remote care. Shock Dampeners were an important part of ambulance vehicles. Of course, Ambulance drones competed with the road ambulances and won in most markets.

Roadside assistance companies such as AAA used to charge people an annual membership and send a tow truck when you run out or gas or get a flat tire when car tires lose pressure or even for silly things such as people locking themselves out of their cars.

AAA, of course, shut down roadside assistance and has changed its business to serve the self-driving cars with pre-planned service based on using data to predict the cars maintenance needs or a car wash. The tow trucks have also become autonomous, but the tow truck drivers offer specialized car maintenance service on-demand.

New Transportation Industry Segments

The concept of a car or truck becoming a connected vehicle led to new industries such as smart parking, Vehicle to Infrastructure Communication, Infotainment, Newer types of connected insurance companies and much more. See the picture from Venture scanner above for a snapshot of the connected transportation segments and players shaping this space in 2017.

5.3 Urban Mobility & City Planning

Cities plan the roads and necessary infrastructure and to administer the necessary regulations to keep the residents safe. Cars played a crucial part in controlling the quality of life of a city because of the traffic they brought and the time people spent circling blocks to find parking. It sets a tone for a city on how rash the citizens drove and establishing the moods of individuals as aggressive as they competed for parking spots.

In 2017, Traffic was a world people could relate to with feelings of frustration. They were under the myth that they could control their commute times by speeding. There used to a police role called 'traffic cop' which is now obsolete. People used to be stopped by these traffic cops and issued a citation and fined. People also parked cars in slots and were given tickets for parking more than 18 inches away from the curb in America. People used to rush out of work meetings and events to top off parking meters manually. First, they automated these parking meters to smart IoT meters. Then they got rid of them once the self-driving cars became prevalent. The cars never extend their parking time limits and pay the city automatically using embedded Blockchain technology.

Urban Mobility was an area of innovation with new autonomous vehicles introduced individuals, seniors and the blind. This was closely tied to city planning. Malls, Public parking lots were freed up, and land use planning became an important topic of discussion for the city and owners of large parking areas. The new urban mobility vehicles had their need for city support.

City infrastructure such as traffic lights, roads, and parking spots became connected Cognitive IoT and communicated with the cars. The city evolved new business models to charge for road use when people used autonomous PODS as workspaces.

It was a time of innovation and transformation that digitized the cities tied closely to the autonomous vehicles. As the self-driving cars piloted the streets of 2017, the city was getting ready to improve the roads, side walks, parking lots, traffic lights, street lamps and more to become cognitive IoT (Internet of Things) to get ready for the autonomous world of 2030.

Chapter 6: BUSINESS MODEL EVOLUTIONS

The big question in 2017 was about the business model for the autonomous world.

What is going to be the successful business model of the self-driving car? Is it ride sharing? Is the auto industry going to switch to a B2B model? Is It something else?

6.1 Ownership: Will Auto Industry switch to B2B?

Self-driving cars led to the speculation on how car ownership will shift with ride-sharing companies. Will consumers stop driving eventually?

Consumers were adopting ride sharing, leading to a demographics ready to not own a car. With it, they did not adopt the pride and loyalty to a piece of metal called a car. With it came their change in behavior to attach mobility and freedom with an asset they keep locked up 95% of the time.

Is the motivation of this segment about not taking up car ownership or is it their aversion to polluting the environment with gas guzzlers? How big was this segment? How fast was it growing? These questions loomed at large in 2017 out into the next decade.

Can we be sure that the millennial who use ride sharing will not switch to owning a car as they switch demographics into being parents or become more affluent with work experience and age? This shared economy data will dictate whether growth in ride sharing will impact consumer auto purchase rates.

If this segment of users is going to ride share, that could explain the growth of electric cars. In 2017 self-driving car growth numbers were mixed up with an assumption that autonomous vehicles were going to be being electric cars. Where did this assumption come from? Imagine this funny scene of a self-driving car, pulling into a gas station and attempting to get gas filled. Now a human will have to serve the self driving car or the gas station has to become robotic to connect with the gas and disperse the gas. Both sound crazy so naturally self-driving cars were being planned as fully electric vehicles.

If you are still staying on that image and wondering how the self-driving electric car recharges itself, look at how the Roomba vacuum cleaner goes back to its charging port or look at a robot that goes back to its geo-fenced charging station in a mall.

Image Credit: Sudha Jamthe. This is the picture of Knightscope, a security robot used in malls in San Jose, California. It is geo-fenced to an area it monitors and goes to the electric port and re-charges itself.

So yes, it is feasible but self driving cars today go home to humans who pamper them with fuel and a lot more moral support for all their disengagements during the day.

The big question remained on whether consumers will not buy self-driving cars and only ride share companies will own cars in the future.

This ownership shift will switch the market from Business to Consumer (B2C) to Business to Business (B2B) with auto makers selling fleets of cars to ride share companies and become commoditized. For this to happen, the shift in ownership has to be a strategic inflection point that has to hit auto and transportation industries like a comet hitting earth. How many times have we seen entire industries switch from B2C to B2B? We have seen companies switch business models from one to another, but that requires changing the employees for new skill set, processes, and systems, marketing as if it is a whole new business.

For this to happen, entire segments of consumers have to change. Race car drivers, families running long weekend vacation trips, parents who shuttle kids on several activities after school, rugged terrain drivers who enjoy the driving and their trucks and a lot more own cars as individual consumers today. They will have to be motivated to switch to a ride-share model. They need a very powerful incentive to make this switch. Such a strong incentive to switch an entire industry to B2B was still missing by 2017.

Autonomous Vehicles are being built on the promise to solve the problem of traffic congestion and loss of life from accidents. In 2017, a Texas A&M research paper challenged the congestion reducing premise of self-driving cars saying that they the autonomous vehicles will drive at speed limit while human drivers adjust the speed to the road speed and usually drive a little above the speed limit. This added to more congestion.

6.2 Ten Futuristic AV Business Models

This brings us back to the b-model question again.

Different business models were tested, some failed, and some evolved over the next ten years.

Here are possible b-models. In 2017 none of these were yet tested.

1. A hybrid model of some segments owning self-driving cars similar to current cars while others using ride share. This begs the design question of whether this population would want the control to drive the car and switch to auto mode when desired. Tesla has proven there is an appetite for this model.

2. Community owned self-driving cars rented or leased on demand by a trustee community that shared the ownership or maintenance cost. A variation is the cost of ownership subsidized by a company who gets access to user data of their mobility habits. e.g., Insero of Denmark developed a community-driven ride-sharing service called Tadaa! and tested this b-model out in 2017.

3. A self-driving car company offering it on short term leases similar to bike rentals in San Francisco? Or a subscription model is also possible here instead of short on-demand trips.

4. Evolution of a service model where self-driving cars are owned by companies who charge for their mobility solution as a service.

e.g., shuttle for students inside a university or golf course or airport. E.g. Auro autonomous shuttles.

5. Will car makers offer mobility services instead of selling the cars? This looks like a viable transformation of b-model for car rental companies such as Hertz or Avis. Instead of renting a car at the airport you pay a service fee for a series of services.

6. Can a retailer subsidize the cost of an autonomous ride for

consumers? Insero's Tadaa! In Denmark tested an innovative business model that allows a retailer like IKEA to pay for a user's ride and learn about their shopping mobility. This business model allows retailers to subsidize trips by treating them as customer acquisition costs and build loyalty of the customer by offering them personalized geo-fenced coupons for their shopping. Another model is for insurance companies to track a fleet of cars and give one to the user instead of their mobility behavior data. Understanding where you go, when, for how long and at what repeat frequency can inform about your risk profile or your shopping behavior.

7. Drive-thru fast food chains were born when people started owning cars and started driving long distance on vacations. Will self-driving cars do the drive through for us? Lyft has added this feature to its rides by mid-2017. But this s not cost effective for a ride share company. A new model has to evolve to replace rest stations and drive thru fast foods to still serve the needs of the self-driving car commuter on a long trip. Maybe drive-through fast food services will deliver the food to self-driving cars if you pre order before you get there.

Maybe rest stations will have to be redesigned with charging stations for the cars and food and restrooms for the humans.

8 The autonomous vehicle becomes a data platform with layers

of services seems to creat an ecosystem of developers building technologies and monetizing services from the car user. The promise of an App store for the car brought in Apple, and Samsung to the car technology business in 2017.

9.. Mobile workplaces could evolve with Autonomous vehicles becoming mobile meeting spaces. This would be a huge disruption of cities as we knew them in 2017. New business models will evolve with cities charging the autonomous mobile workplaces a tax for using their roads. I share my vision for such mobile workplaces later in Chapter 11.

10. Open-source Car Cognition technologies were developed in 2017. It is possible that such add-on Car Cognition technologies could become commercially available to make human-driven cars into autonomous vehicles. Though this is possible, I will not bet on this becoming a business of scale.

6.3 Autonomous Vehicle Business Framework

The Autonomous Vehicle is set to disrupt multiple industries as we discussed earlier. There is no set path to this disruption before we reach the fully driverless world with fully autonomous vehicles. This road is full of opportunities for entrepreneurs and business innovators to create new businesses and shape the Driverless World.

Here is the Autonomous Vehicle Business Framework that I have developed and teach my Stanford CSP students at "The Business of Self-Driving Cars" class.

Autonomous Vehicle Business Framework

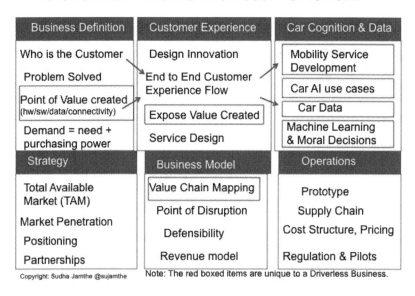

Business Definition	Customer Experience	Car Cognition & Data
Who is the Customer	Design Innovation	Mobility Service Development
Problem Solved	End to End Customer Experience Flow	Car AI use cases
Point of Value created (hw/sw/data/connectivity)	Expose Value Created	Car Data
Demand = need + purchasing power	Service Design	Machine Learning & Moral Decisions
Strategy	**Business Model**	**Operations**
Total Available Market (TAM)	Value Chain Mapping	Prototype
Market Penetration	Point of Disruption	Supply Chain
Positioning	Defensibility	Cost Structure, Pricing
Partnerships	Revenue model	Regulation & Pilots

Copyright: Sudha Jamthe @sujamthe   Note: The red boxed items are unique to a Driverless Business.

My autonomous vehicle business framework is a guide for entrepreneurs and corporate innovators to create a new business. The new business could be in the Automotive or Transportation space. It could be in any industry disrupted by the autonomous vehicle such as medical, retail, insurance, freight, farming, construction, mining, tourism, medical, logistics, warehouses, new mobility services and more.

The framework starts with the business definition and guides on product management, market development, business model development, unique to AV opportunities such as creating businesses using Car data and Car AI cognition technologies, design, launch strategy and operations. Wishing you success in creating new disruptive businesses.

Chapter 7 Mobility Services & Disruptions

The autonomous vehicle is not about making our cars and truck drive themselves without a human driver. It is a fundamental shift in urban mobility as known for 100 years.

7.1 Personal Mobility Solutions

Ford and Honda launched pilots of personal mobility vehicles as autonomous single human mobility options. It was speculative whether people were going green not owning multi-user cars and still needed a personal mobility vehicle and what were the use-cases that would evolve.

The real promise of the shift in mobility from autonomous vehicles was in the promise to bring newer demographics of people to become mobile such as visually impaired people or senior citizens who could not drive cars.

7.2 Mobility Services

The data in the connected cars offered a wealth of options for Car Manufacturers (OEMs) and several technology start-ups to offer mobility services.

Mobility services known as Mobility as a Service (MAAS) was a service offering that helped the user with new conveniences that was not possible before connected vehicles with precious data about the car and the user. After-sales-service changed to a predictive model where the car informed the service shop when it needed maintenance and proactively scheduled itself for maintenance. The autonomous vehicle drove itself for service adapting to the working schedule of its human passenger.

OEMs could offer Infotainment and digital streaming services with an awareness of the human passengers needs as the car drove the user to their multiple destinations. Each usage of the car gave data about the user's behavior and mobility patterns creating a wealth of services. For example, an autonomous vehicle collected data and knew the regular timings when a user commuted to work and their habits to stop at certain destinations or follow certain routes. They knew when the user used the vehicle for entertainment or work. This enabled mobility service offerings that were personalized to the user, saving them money and time.

As the car developed more cognition with a car AI, it also learned the user's emotional response to geo-fencing deals and various stimuli in their infotainment needs. All this gave room to a broad range of mobility services.

When cars began to use Blockchain technologies, it gave more option for mobility service because cars could make payments for a user's services based on a trusted distributed ledger. For example, an autonomous vehicle could offer to self-park itself after dropping the user and pay for its service using Blockchain. The car could become smarter about available parking spaces and best cost by negotiating with other cars and parking garages remotely.

Innovation in Mobility Services was a huge opportunity equally available to Auto OEMs and businesses big and small.

SUDHA JAMTHE

Chapter 8 Changing Jobs Landscape

8.1 Autonomous Vehicle Product Managers

The role of the Autonomous Vehicles Product Manager began to boom in 2017. The role of the Product Manager is a pivotal role in Technology. Product Managers build the product flows and optimal integration points. They are necessary to adapt to how autonomous vehicles change the product's interaction with customers and create new customer segments and price sentiments. Technology product managers and domain expert business managers from Automotive and Transportation industries came to learn about autonomous vehicle technology, and changing customer demands to fill these new Product Manager roles.

8.2 Machine Learning and Car Informatics Jobs

AI engineers who can master machine learning and deep learning algorithms are surely at the forefront of building out the technology platforms needed to run the self-driving cars. As cars stored data to make decisions and data about the state of the vehicle and the consumer behavior of its usage, the field of Car Informatics boomed with demand for more data scientists and data savvy business managers who could build infotainment and other usage services for the evolving car customers.

8.3 Policy Makers, Designers & Dealers

As the Federal Highway safety departments, cities teamed up with carmakers and autonomous vehicle technology academics and industry players. There was a boom in need for lawyers and policy makers.

As the autonomous car technology began developing to become more reliable and safe, industrial and service designer jobs scaled up. Automakers started figuring out the shift and demands of customers for various autonomous vehicles. Even car dealers had to become tech savvy to educate consumers on features of the connected cars and when they could safely switch to driver assisted autonomous driving mode.

CHAPTER 9 REGULATION

A partnership of government agencies, academic researchers, private technology companies and automobile companies addressed the challenges to get us from 2017 to the Driverless world of 2030. New challenges that will continue to be solved even in 2030 are Safety, Privacy, Liability, Security, Reliability, Licensing, and Insurance.

9.1 Regulation and Compliance

It all started with the agreement of the definition of an Autonomous Vehicles. National Highway Transportation Safety Patrol (NHTSA) the US Federal organization accepted the definition of 5 levels of autonomous vehicles as defined by SEA.

This definition of the autonomous vehicle became the golden standard to compare any autonomous vehicle that wanted to do real roadways testing to offer a license to operate on the roads ensuring public safety.

LEVELS OF DRIVING AUTOMATION
From SAE J3016™ adopted by NHTSA Federal Automated Vehicle Policy, Sep 2016)

Level 5 - Full Automation: Automated Driving System controls all dynamic driving task under all roadway and environmental conditions similar to what a human can do.

Level 4 - High Automation: Automated Driving System controls all dynamic driving tasks even if a human does not intervene when requested.

Level 3 - Conditional Automation: Automated Driving System controls all dynamic driving tasks but a human can intervene when requested.

Level 2 - Partial Automation Multiple Driver assistance systems of steering and acceleration/deceleration using driving environment info

Level 1 - Driver-Assistance: Driver assistance system of steering or acceleration/deceleration using driving environment info

Level 0 - No Automation.

© Sudha Jamthe

IoTDisruptions.com   http://bit.ly/IoTAIBook   © sujamthe | 9

Image Credit: Sudha Jamthe. Levels of driving automation was developed by SAE and adopted by the USA NHTSA Federal Automated Vehicle Policy in Sep 2016.

The California DMV (Department of Motor Vehicles) clearly defines what is not an autonomous vehicle to differentiate from the various driver assistance autonomous features of human-driven cars. It states that "An autonomous vehicle does not include a vehicle that has one or more collision avoidance systems, such as electronic blind spot assistance, automated emergency braking systems, park assist, adaptive cruise control, lane keep assist, lane departure warning, and traffic jam and queuing assist." These come under Level 2 of automation, but the vehicle is not treated as an autonomous vehicle and does not require an autonomous vehicle testing permit.

Nevada was the first American state to allow autonomous vehicles to operate. California, Florida, Louisiana, Michigan, North Dakota, Tennessee and Utah and Washington D.C. followed this. Massachusetts and Arizona joined by the executive order by the Governor.

In 2017, the focus was on Technology and public safety. There were open questions about who was liable if the self-driving car met with an accident and caused loss of people or property.

In 2013, DMV California set out to create the regulatory framework to allow self-driving vehicles to drive autonomously for testing on real roads. It imposed a $5Mil insurance and requires a human driver at the driver's seat of testing vehicles as a starting point to address the liability issue.

In Nov 2016, Insurance Institute of Highway Safety issued a special Autonomous Vehicles Report and said crash test dummies were not going to retire with self-driving cars anytime soon.

In Dec 2016 Uber had a standoff with the city of San Francisco running its Autonomous Cars without an Autonomous Vehicle License from the city and stopped after the Attorney General issued a cease and desist.

The challenge for regulators is still that driverless vehicles technology is opaque. There is no explicit model for regulators to validate when a company claims it is ready for road test. In early 2017 there were 20 companies running roadside tests and this expanded to 33 within the first quarter of the year. There is a looming question which might sound like science fiction. When the vehicle becomes fully autonomous and can make independent decisions on the road, who should be regulated, the driver or fleet owner or the Cognitive Car itself?

In 2017 with 2020 as the promising year when autonomous vehicles are promised by top automakers, the regulators had to cater to what were they going to offer regulation to drive independently on the road? It appeared as if different automakers were considering to release different levels of autonomous vehicles at Level 2 or Level 3 by 2020. These could be shuttles of fixed path vehicles. There was speculation of a separate autonomous vehicle lane in the highways. But this did not have the regulation support in terms of public good justification.

Some car companies were already adding autonomous features into their human driven cars. For example Audi had a model which offered lane assist which was the basic feature for an autonomous vehicle. Tesla offered the driver a choice to switch to Auto mode and did not start with a license as an autonomous vehicle like Google. Fleets were being tested to run in platooning mode where a group of vehicles followed one vehicle which made driving decisions. These offer challenges for regulars to develop the right regulatory framework for autonomous vehicles without stifling their innovation while keeping the public safe.

In August 2017 US, US House of Representatives (Congress) unanimously passed the SELF DRIVE bill and awaited support from the US Senate. This bill let autonomous vehicles to self-assess their safety performance and limit states from imposing performance regulations. It also mandated self-driving cars to report on how they plan to manage cyber-security and about data collected to protect privacy of users. The bill removed some safety standards that were applicable to human driven cars such as steering wheels. The House bill covered cars and did not include trucks. In case you are curious, SELF DRIVE bill stands for 'Safely Ensuring Lives Future Deployment and Research In Vehicle Evolution Act'.

Overall 2017 saw the regulation debate turn removing friction from companies to innovating in autonomous vehicles space.

9.2 Security, Privacy & Interoperability

Tesla partnered with BMW and created a global standard in electric vehicle charges. The autonomous vehicle software and hardware in 2017 was still built in isolation by competing companies without any interoperable standards. Google after piloting the self-driving car with other car manufacturer's cars for eight years, decided it was going to make the automobile hardware to work with its software AI. Ford invested in the startup Argo AI to help develop competing Car AI software.

Comma.ai put its technology to make a car hardware and software out in open source in 2016. Some startups offered retrofitted camera that a consumer can turn select car models into autonomous vehicles.

Udacity set out with the first self-driving class for engineers and put the algorithms in Open source, which paved the way to create an open standard, and discussion for the technologists to build upon each other's work. This open source car created new questions about the liability of an autonomous vehicle created by open source software contributed by many developers globally.

V2V (Vehicle to Vehicle) communication once mandated by the US Government, forced companies to share minimum information to facilitate communication between autonomous cars. V2V Communication had to evolve over many years to create interoperable cognitive communication Car AI software. It made the roads safe for everyone and reduced the risk for automakers.

SUDHA JAMTHE

CHAPTER 10 Insurance Disruptions

"Automation and Driverless vehicles will bring with them a foundational change in insurance. Blockchain, AI, and other technologies will play a vital role in offering contextual coverage and shift ownership for coverage between manufacturer, fleet owner, driver, or user of the vehicle. All of this opens the door to a new digital generation of insurance." – **Mike CEO, SVIA Insurance's 1ˢᵗ Open Innovation Accelerator & Conference Chair at InsurTech Silicon Valley**

Insurance is another industry, connected cars, and autonomous vehicles are set to disrupt.

Who is liable for the damages of a driverless car? What will be the insurance and ownership models of shared economies leading to unmanned vehicles like drones and self-service robots? When a driver switches a car to autonomous driving mode, does it transfer the risk from the driver to the car manufacturer? If so, how can insurance companies manage their liabilities and keep the drivers and cars safe?

Insurance is an industry focused on measuring the risk of a person for auto, life, health or home. Gartner had predicted in 2016 that consumers would wear 411 million wearable devices. These devices tracked a person's health and fitness and produced huge volumes of behavioral data. By 2017, people were adopting smart devices in their home. Cars were becoming connected cars too. These devices were creating conveniences that could prolong life, change the behavior of users regarding their interaction and maintenance of their home, auto, and their bodies. The most critical part of the autonomous car disruption for insurance comes from the vast volume of data about the customer. This data can inform consumer behavior and help insurance build better risk models and manage claims process in an automated way. Insurance companies could also become life coaches to guide the user positively with their data.

But first, business leaders in insurance industry had to figure out whether to insure the car or the driver because technically, the human in a driverless car is not a driver, she is a passenger.

10.1 Insure the driver or the car?

The driverless car was in pilot mode in 2017. Autonomous vehicles pilots received stringent Insurance regulations. Initially, there was confusion about who will bear the risk of a collision or injury during an autonomous vehicle testing on public roads. This confusion was because technology companies such as Google made the autonomous vehicle technology and Lexus or Volvo and other manufacturers made the cars. The State DMVs which followed the definitions from NHTSA of the USA defined the 'manufacturers' as the maker of the autonomous vehicle technology or a car maker who built a self-driving vehicle ground up or someone who modified an existing vehicle to make it autonomous. This entity had to apply and get the testing licenses and pay for the surety bond of $5 Million per vehicle and purchase an autonomous vehicle Insurance.

Tesla got out of this risk by passing the risk onto the drivers by asking them to make the decision when to switch to auto-pilot and to be alert to take control back. So in the 2016 Tesla auto-pilot accident, where the driver died from a truck crash, the driver was blamed for negligence as he was watching a movie in the autonomous car without paying notice to the road. Uber attempted to argue with the city of California in Dec 2016, that its driverless pilot did not fit the definition of an autonomous vehicle pilot and hence it did not require an autonomous vehicle permit. Uber received a cease-and-desist from the attorney general of San Francisco to stop driving its driverless pilot after a minor accident at a red light which luckily did not harm anyone.

The government had to walk a tightrope between regulation for safety and not stifle innovation of autonomous vehicles. There was competition between different states within the USA inviting companies to run their driverless pilots. Uber moved from California to Alaska to continue its driverless pilots in 2017.

A new set of players such as Udacity and Comma.ai evolved to create open source self-driving cars technology. Udacity created a team of developers globally who built upon each other's work and created an autonomous car software and hardware. This open source car added more questions about who should insure the autonomous car for risk and safety.

Out of Pilot mode in 2021

The real questions on insurance ownership began as we got closer to 2021, the year, major car makers had promised a self-driving car for sale. The question debated was about the definition of what made up the driverless car and what business models would evolve regarding car ownership. If a company purchased the vehicle and gave it out for ride-sharing to different consumers, that company could buy insurance for the car. If the individual users were going to own the self-driving cars, as was the expectation in 2017, then there were two stakeholders involved. The manufacturer or maker of the autonomous vehicle and the owner or purchaser of the vehicle. The car owner may or may not be the passenger riding the driverless car.

In 2017, since the common thinking was that the autonomous vehicle was going to learn to operate entirely independently and safely, there was no consideration of the car communicating with the passenger or the human driver or city infrastructure. Communication with the passenger was considered a nice-to-have to offer a comfortable environment and entertainment for the passenger of the car. The car did not have an intelligent AI that could interact with the passenger. The passenger was perceived as a silent player not impacting the car's safety on the road. The car maker assumed all the risk of the driverless car. Consumer auto insurance industry feared the loss of insurance business expecting to stop insuring people as they stopped being drivers and switched to become passengers of autonomous vehicles.

In the next decade, the car developed the Car AI, and the driverless car began communicating with passengers, pedestrians, city infrastructure and the human in the driver-driven car. At this point, the passenger could make decisions that impacted how the driverless car interacted with human driven cars on the road. At that time, the passenger created risks to the autonomous car and had to bear the insurance risk.

In 2017, this disrupted the consumer car insurance business with losses with each consumer adopting driverless car and becoming an autonomous vehicle passenger.

Soon, this led to interesting business models with autonomous car makers partnering with insurance companies to offer insurance to its buyers be it ride-share businesses or individuals.

As car software players evolved as new businesses, the insurance companies were tasked with separating the car's mechanical parts, different from the autonomous vehicle layer of sensors and software as provided by two players. For example, Ford invested in Aero.ai. Ford makes the car hardware and mechanical parts. Aero.ai creates the software that makes the car run as an autonomous car. This partnership of automaker and car AI software companies creates a tiered layer of ownership to different parts of the car. Hence this leads to a tiered layer of insurance responsibility too.

10.2 Can we sue an algorithm?

2017 was just the start of the world getting automated with algorithms for everything from scheduling, to shopping to travel planning. BMW in 2016 shared a 'Next 100 Vision' with an Augmented reality dashboard and 'companion' an algorithm what they quote as "symbolizes the intelligence, connectivity and availability" of the car that can perform autonomous routine tasks or give advice to the driver.

With algorithms, the question arose on who is in charge and who bears the risks? Companies build algorithms by feeding data to the programs. Ted Friedman of Gartner tweeted in 2016 saying, "With the rise of algorithmic business, data governance must address not only data quality but also the quality of algorithms."

What does it mean to have quality governance similar to data governance? Data about users tells about our behavior more than we want to share, invading our privacy and breaking compliance required in some industries such as insurance, healthcare, and online marketing.

Can a bad quality algorithm harm us?

The algorithm can give us bad advice. With a self-driving car, it could make bad decisions and drive erratically. As long as it follows the government regulation to drive safely at Level 5 automation, we are still safe.

A bad algorithm may be a poorly written algorithm that breaks into our privacy. It could learn our habits and misuse that data. It could hold us hostage to a particular service by saving our friend's contacts. It could spam our friends in our name without our permission. It could sell our behavioral information to companies. It could offer to help us shop better but serve the retailer or travel provider. That is not bad quality that is outright dishonest business practice. All this adds to the risk of the car or the algorithmic business and creates an unprecedented challenge for the insurance company.

So checking the quality of an algorithm seems to be about ensuring that the algorithm follows privacy and data usage policies that applies to humans and to make sure its business model is one of honesty and integrity. It is about checking these for the people and firms that develop and control these algorithms.

10.3 Contextual Real-Time Insurance

By 2017, Insurance companies with usage-based insurance gave drivers a 2-inch dongle device to plug into a car's dashboard to collect location and driving data. TomTom's Coordina, Metromile Pulse from Mobile Devices of France, Progressive's Snapshop are dongle based insurance vendors. They collected data about the driving behavior of the driver and could build accurate risk models to adjust insurance premiums. GE built-in such a dongle in its car in 2017, to collect driving behavior data but offered it as a choice for the driver to opt to share this with insurance companies.

Cars have data on actual driving behavior tied to time and

location. In 2017, this was not easy to export out of the vehicles. Over the years with autonomous vehicles, this began to be used to make claims and disputes accurate, saving valuable time.

Contextual real-time insurance is on the verge to become a reality. Car AI could now also switch who was responsible for the insurance coverage in real-time. Here is an example of the contextual switch of real-time coverage from Michael Conner, CEO of Silicon Valley Insurance Accelerator (SVIA). With a fleet of driverless vans, the owner of the fleet was responsible for insurance when it was loaded correctly and doing a delivery. If the user of the vehicle did not load it correctly and used it in hazardous areas known for vandalism, negligently, the responsibility switched to the user of the van. If some sensors on the van were not functioning properly, while driving autonomously, the van responsibility shifted to the van maker. If the user decided to switch out of autonomous mode and drove the vehicle manually, in some situation, she bears the responsibility of the insurance.

The consumers had to tradeoff insurance premiums for the privacy of their driving data. Insurance companies wanted to make this a positive experience for their customers.

Over the next decade, wearables on the commuters' body began to communicate with the Car AI. There was the looming possibility that these wearables could be nanobots swimming inside a human body or an implant that enhanced their brain. Either way, they offered data about the people inside the car. When car communication became more prevalent, the car AI could communicate with the human's data.

The insurance companies took the leadership to transform their business from one that talked about negative things to their customer to become a life coach that guided a user's risk choices using data from the driverless cars and other IoT.

CHAPTER 11 My Predictions: 2030 to 2050 & Beyond

As you enter this chapter, let me warn you. We are looking at the road ahead for the fully connected world from 2030 to 2050 and beyond. The futurist in me is fully awake and dreaming up scenarios of a world beyond our imagination.

11.1 Mobile Workplace PODS

In 2017, Apple was speculated to enter the driverless scene by 2020. They introduced Augmented Reality in cars, which soon became a standard feature of how we interacted with a car. I predict a revolution in driverless cars called PODS, a customizable, modular self-driving car. It creates a platform for automobile manufacturers but also for developers to build out modules of hardware and software to adapt the vehicle to do different things for different consumers. The PODS would make the autonomous vehicle into a mobile building, which a user can change to whatever they want to do with their autonomous cars – mobile health clinic, mobile hair salon, mobile office pods, portable coffee shop, etc. This would create new small businesses, which will replace Main Street as a mobile set of autonomous vehicle pods that come to us instead of us going to a fixed street. The PODS would create a mobile workplace for teams to meet and manage the logistics of picking up different team members for face to face interactions while it drives along the most optimal path to pick up or drop off the next person.

The city will have to adapt to PODS, and they will start charging rent for using the roads as these mobile businesses circled. It will bring back the small town feel on wheels and also allow us to free up space to create more green spaces.

11.2 Addressing Inequality

In 2017 the world was facing more income inequality than the past years. Self-driving cars by design are reliant on the road infrastructure to train the software for the car to drive safely. So countries with poor infrastructure were left behind. This will motivate them to adopt drones faster than autonomous cars and trucks. Autonomous drones from Zipline did medical delivery in war-torn Rwanda, and the drones from Matternet did freight delivery in rugged mountains of Nepal. After the self-driving cars serve the metro population, they will improve their technology to run in rough terrains and adapt to poor infrastructure environments. They will also build out connected infrastructure like connected pavements with sensors, so it was a 2-way innovation that will feed upon each other in developing countries. Developing countries will also force the development of the technology to be more autonomous, requiring less trained personnel, low power consumption and easy set up by untrained professionals making it more user-friendly. It will also expedite the innovation with the focus on different problems. In Africa, the focus is not on traffic and commute but food equality and bringing the electric grid sharing from multi-family solar grids to optimize green energy across a wider geography. This will lead to focus on autonomous freight delivery of food and smart trucks that keep food safe. It will result in autonomous vehicles that do Vehicle to Vehicle communication to share power when a critical autonomous vehicle carrying medicine loses power and another driving nearby could help by power sharing.

The same applies to visually impaired. The self-driving car features of 2017 used to have driver-set Autopilot modes which expected the driver to let the car run autonomously but watch and jump in if there was an emergency situation. By 2030 the self-driving car companies will innovate for visually impaired. This will give the opportunity for entrepreneurs to use sensors to create way finders for the blind for cities. My prediction is that they will build out self-driving cars for the visually impaired to interact with the car using voice and augmented reality making it a more natural interaction instead of a forced interaction with a computer. The car will identify them by biometrics and give them much needed mobility.

11.3 A Car for Kids

In 2017, parents were sold minivans saying the lower step was comfortable for women to enter the car in suits as they drove their children to soccer and the vans were fitted with a TV screen for entertainment when they drove long distance. Slowly kids were given an iPad each in the back seat making the TVs obsolete. Still, soccer moms (and some dads) drove kids to games and after school activities.

With self-driving cars, parents will have a new solution to safely let their children move between locations with an autonomous driving car door locked by the parent. There is much innovation needed to resolve the issues of access to the car to let kids in and out and to deal with road emergency situations. This will create a new class of kid-friendly vehicles that is colorful, fun and a safe and an appealing place for kids to drive autonomously, controlled by their parents. The automotive makers who figure this out to come out with fancy models and add new gaming gears in the car are going to win a whole new category of personal vehicles.

11.4 Human Computer Interface

Moral Machines

As our world becomes more autonomous with intelligent machines including self-driving cars, it is important to be aware that we are giving autonomous decision-making in the hands of machines. Humans train these machines and give it the training data to build models to use to make decisions. They unknowingly include their biases in this data teaching the machines their biases.

One classic problem debated among experts is called the "Trolley Problem" where a trolley has to decide to switch between two paths with both of them killing some number of people.

MIT set up a Moral Machines site (http://moralmachine.mit.edu/) where we can choose between two scenarios of decisions by a crashing self-driving car based on the knowledge of who will get killed. It is set up as a crowd-sourced site to collect human perspectives on moral decisions made by intelligent machines such as self-driving cars.

One business question to ask is whether a self-driving car company should expose its moral decision capabilities and how will it impact the customer's decisions to choose their car over their competition. But there is no winning in this path. Will your customers buy a machine that has a high moral compass or will they shun buying a self-driving car that admits killing its passengers to save pedestrian lives?

We have to look at this problem in perspective of our own driving experiences. The reality is that crashes happen by negligent and drunk drivers and it's a very rare for us to face such moral dilemmas when we drive today in 2017 as human drivers. Such questions are raised as theoretical options with our fear or letting go and giving control to an intelligent machine that will make decisions as we sit trustingly in high-speed roads shared by many other speeding machines.

So our focus should be on building self-driving cars to be absolutely safe to drive following road rules, and able to adapt to surprise scenarios on the road equal to, not more than what we expect of humans today.

Our changing relationship with Intelligent Machines

The question remains about our changing relationship with intelligent machines including the self-driving vehicles.

Our experiences are nuanced and filtered by context, identity, and relevance based on location and time. This is influenced by our moods and our biases that are stored deep in our lizard brains controlling how we feel, perceive reality, get creative, solve problems, define and store as memory. Our experiences and recalling them shapes our identity of who we are and helps us grow in self-awareness. This underlying ability to live our experience as life is human intelligence. Add free will to it, and it creates many billion unique combinations making it complicated to replicate the human experience and human cognition. So we thought.

As we get comfortable with autonomous vehicles driving us, it is not going to be a 'thing' that is at our call to drive us around. Our dependence on intelligent machines including our cars will blur our sense of the reality of who is in-charge.

How will our relationship with the machine change as it smartens up deep learning the other computer's behavior and begins to advise us? There is research going on about how our interaction with devices will change our behavior with other humans as a society. We can see this reality only when we get closer to a fully autonomous world.

Affective computing teaches machines to understand emotions with the goal to develop empathy to help them fit in socially and to take actions based on sensing our emotions. Wize Mirror from Semeoticons, a project from the Italian National Research Council, measures a person's overall health from facial recognition. The AI promised in the "The Next 100 years" from BMW may very well do that.

When our car reminds us to manage our temper, in our self-interest to help us maintain good health, we may be crossing that line where our sense of control may shift to the car.

CHAPTER 12 Conclusion

We are lucky to be living in 2017, the transformational year of the Driverless car. We get to shape the next 15 years to build the Driverless world of 2030 and beyond. We get to build out the car AI for the Driverless car to learn road communications. We get to be that special generation that transitions between driving our cars to experience being a passenger in a Driverless car.

We own the business transformation of several industries most notably, Automotive and Transportation. We get to shape our city of 2030 by redesigning our infrastructure to become smart Cognitive IoT that communicates with the car. We get to design the future of mobility.

As entrepreneurs and corporate innovators, you get to dream with me to iterate new designs, develop new business models, and build new businesses and markets to get us to 2030.

We get to reshape urban mobility and define a whole new way of working in mobile workplaces. We get to plan landscape design strategies as the autonomous vehicle impacts parking and land usage patterns for malls, offices and city centers.

Finally, we get to create a new chapter in the human-machine interface on how we are going to share the world with the Cognitive AI machines we build in the car, city, and wearables on our bodies.

Here's to your success creating the Driverless world of 2030.

Please share this book with your friends and fellow innovators on Facebook, LinkedIn, Twitter, ProductHunt and instagram. Post a review on Amazon. Contact the author with feedback and to share your unique challenges and successes at http://driverlessworldbook.com

Appendix 1: Autonomous Vehicle Pilots in 2017

As of August 2017, CA DMV has issued Autonomous Vehicle Testing Permits to the following entities:

- **Volkswagen Group of America, Inc**
- **Mercedes Benz Research & Development North America, Inc**
- **Google Auto, LLC/Waymo**
- **Delphi Automotive Systems, LLC**
- **Tesla Motors, Inc.**
- **Bosch, LLC**
- **Nissan North America, Inc**
- **GM Cruise LLC**
- **BMW**
- **Honda**
- **Ford**
- Zoox, Inc.
- Drive.ai, Inc.
- Faraday & Future Inc.
- Baidu USA LLC
- Wheego Electric Cars Inc.
- Valeo North America, Inc.
- NextEV USA, Inc.
- Telenav, Inc.
- NVIDIA Corporation

- Otto – the autonomous truck (owned by Uber in dispute with Google Alphabet Inc over its technology ownership as of Aug 2017)
- Apple
- CivilMaps Inc. test drives its Car Cognition product.
- Samsung

The highlighted companies in the list above continued their pilot from 2016 and submitted a Disengagement report to DMV in Jan 2017.

Global pilots and ride-share/shutte/mobility Pilots

- Cruise Automation (https://www.getcruise.com/) , part of GM, began testing an autonomous ride-share service in San Francisco for its employees using Chevolet Bolt EVs.
- Nutonomy, the autonomous car technology from MIT has been tested in self-driving taxis in Singapore and Dubai. In late 2017, Nutonomy and Lyft have partnered to offer self-driving ride-sharing in Boston, USA.
- Samsung tested autonomous driving with Hyundai cars in South Korea and helped Renault with its self-driving car technology.
- GATEway shuttles and Lutz Pods are being tested in UK.
- Honda UX- 3 Powered by ASIMO Robotics technology (launched in CES 2017)
- Ford Carr- E (launched in Mobile World Congress 2017
- Einride of Sweden created a pilot T-Pod driverless truck for transportation and promised 200 pods running in Sweden between Gothenburg and Helsingborg by 2020.

Appendix 2: Driverless Cognitive AI Research References

'Parallel autonomy and autonomous cars, CSAIL-Toyota joint research effort'. By Javier Alonso-Mora, (MIT Computer Science and Artificial Intelligence Lab CSAIL)

MIT Prof Picards' work on Affective Deep Learning

Stanford Race car Shelley

SAIL- Toyota AI research at Stanford http://aicenter.stanford.edu

Safe Feedback Interactions in Human-Autonomous Vehicle Systems http://aicenter.stanford.edu/safe-feedback-interactions-in-human-autonomous-vehicle-systems/

Resolving Multiplexed Automotive Communications: Applied Agency and the Social Car by Sally Applin and Michael Fischer published in IEEE.

The Race to 2021: The State of Autonomous Vehicles and a 'Who's Who' of Industry Drivers," tracks 80 companies in 11 categories across 19 market applications.

SUDHA JAMTHE

Bibliography

Statistics Reference

Commuter Congestion Stats

Texas A&M Transportation Institute and INRIX, "2015 Urban Mobility Scorecard," August 2015. https://tti.tamu.edu/2015/08/26/traffic-gridlock-sets-new-records-for-traveler-misery/

(NHTSA) National Highway Traffic Safety Administration, Fatality Analysis Reporting System (FARS) Data, (https://www-fars.nhtsa.dot.gov/Main/ index.aspx

Warehouses in America https://www.bls.gov/iag/tgs/iag493.htm

Gartner Press Release 2013 estimated 26 Billion devices & Cisco estimates 50Bil devices by 2020https://www.cisco.com/.../IoT_IBSG_0411FINAL.pdf

Autonomous Car Sensor Market Growth by 2030 https://www.statista.com/statistics/423106/projected-global-market-for-autonomous-driving-sensor-components/

Projected Autonomous car revenues by 2021 https://www.statista.com/statistics/472381/projected-autonomous-driving-revenue-in-the-us/

Wearables market size http://www.gartner.com/newsroom/id/3198018

US Self-Driving Car Pilots

http://www.nytimes.com/2016/07/01/business/self-driving-tesla-fatal-crash-investigation.html?_r=0

Automotive company plans on releasing a self-driving car stats
https://www.statista.com/chart/7009/self-driving-cars-are-on-their-way/

Autonomous Truck and Industry Vehicles Pilots

Otto, self driving truck makes autonomous delivery in Oct 2016 in Colorado https://www.wired.com/2016/10/ubers-self-driving-truck-makes-first-delivery-50000-beers/

http://www.cat.com/en_US/by-industry/mining/surface-mining/surface-technology/command/command-for-hauling.html

Platooning Trucks

https://www.eutruckplatooning.com/About/Corridors+to+drive+MAP/default.aspx

https://www.eutruckplatooning.com/News/844450.aspx

UK Truck Platooning Proposal reactions
https://www.ukhaulier.co.uk/news/road-transport/platooning/latest-industry-views-on-the-news-self-driving-truck-platooning-trial-in-the-uk/

https://www.usspecial.com/michigan-law-opens-a-door-for-platooning-2/

http://articles.sae.org/15527/

http://www.ttnews.com/articles/volvo-trucks-start-european-platoon-demonstration-tour

Connected Cars Uses and Security

http://www.cnet.com/news/movimento-ota-mitsubishi-infotainment/

http://www.wired.com/2015/10/five-car-hacking-lessons-we-learned-this-summer/ (car hacks)

Autonomous Vehicle Regulations

America's NHTSA Federal Automated Vehicles Policy
https://one.nhtsa.gov/nhtsa/av/av-policy.html#_en46

Vehicle to Vehicle (V2V) Communication mandate from NHTSA (Dec 13 2016)
https://www.nhtsa.gov/press-releases/us-dot-advances-deployment-connected-vehicle-technology-prevent-hundreds-thousands

Autonomous Vehicle Information Library
http://www.aamva.org/Autonomous-Vehicle-Information-Library/

Autonomous Vehicle Deployment in California
https://www.dmv.ca.gov/portal/dmv/detail/vr/autonomous/auto

American Autonomous Vehicle Legislation
http://www.ncsl.org/research/transportation/autonomous-vehicles-legislation.aspx

SELF DRIVE bill (USA) https://www.wired.com/story/congress-self-driving-car-law-bill

Europe Self Driving Car Pilots

Volvo 'Drive Me' self driving car pilot in London in early 2017http://www.telegraph.co.uk/business/2016/04/26/look-no-hands-driverless-volvos-to-hit-britains-streets/

Driverless car pilots in Europe
http://www.telegraph.co.uk/cars/features/how-do-driverless-cars-work/

Roborace launched its Robocar at MWC's 'Connected Vehicles' keynote, by CEO Denis Sverdlov
https://www.mobileworldlive.com/featured-content/top-three/roborace-to-give-connected-vehicles-a-boost/

Lutz Pathfinder https://www.autoblog.com/2015/02/12/the-lutz-pathfinder-pod-uk-first-driverless-car-video/

GATEway
https://gateway-project.org.uk/the-gateway-project-announces-the-next-phase-of-driverless-pod-trials/

Roboat in Amsterdam
http://senseable.mit.edu/roboat/

Technology - what a self-driving car sees

Tesla Model S Autopilot Forward Collision Warning at Work
http://www.businessinsider.com/tesla-avoids-accident-before-happens-2016-12

How Tesla Auto Pilot Works

http://www.whatafuture.com/2014/06/14/google-driverless-car-the-obstacle-detection-unit/

Gateway Airport Shuttle in UK Greenwich Peninsula May 2016

Shirish Jamthe's Open source Github on Self-driving car computer vision and Deep Learning models

Waleed Abdulla's Open source Github on Traffic Sign recognition with TensorFlow. His github has other CNN and Deep Learning work.

Driving Simulator Labs

http://www.umtri.umich.edu/what-we-offer/driving-simulator

https://www.nads-sc.uiowa.edu/

http://lctr.eng.fiu.edu/DrivingSimulator.htm

Many design decisions

https://www.washingtonpost.com/local/trafficandcommuting/self-driving-cars-reach-a-fork-in-the-road-and-automakers-take-different-routes/2016/08/24/5cdeaba8-63d9-11e6-8b27-bb8ba39497a2_story.html?utm_term=.a10542879146

Industry Analysis

Altimeter State of Autonomous Vehicles Whos-who-Report
https://www.slideshare.net/Altimeter/the-race-to-2021-the-state-of-autonomous-vehicles-and-a-whos-who-of-industry-drivers/1

Understanding Standards

https://transportevolved.com/2014/06/16/nissan-bmw-look-adopt-teslas-charging-standard/

The Car Connectivity Consortium (CCC)
http://carconnectivity.org/

SAE On-Road Automated Driving (ORAD) Committee

Business models

Dominoes tests pizza delivery with self-driving cars
http://money.cnn.com/2017/09/01/technology/future/free-transportation-self-driving-cars/index.html

Transportation Innovations

T-pods from Einride http://mashable.com/2017/07/06/einride-self-driving-truck-t-pod-reveal/#LpmMPb98Qgqx

Auto Tech Platform Business

Samsung   joining   self-driving   car   testing   in CA http://www.bbc.com/news/technology-41122102

Moral Machines

MIT's Moral Machines' survey - http://moralmachine.mit.edu/

Artificial Intelligence and Futuristic Technologies

http://www.theguardian.com/technology/2014/dec/09/synapse-ibm-neural-computing-chip

http://amitsheth.blogspot.com/2015/03/smart-iot-iot-as-human-agent-human.html

More references

Stanford One Hundred Year study on AI https://ai100.stanford.edu/2016-report (ADD TO COGNTIVE IOT BOOK)

http://hackaday.com/2017/01/12/at-last-an-open-source-electric-vehicle-from-a-major-manufacturer/

http://press.renault.co.uk/press-release/fb984a0e-7b5e-4f09-9c17-02fb185bd49d

http://www.inc.com/kevin-j-ryan/how-tesla-is-using-ai-to-make-self-driving-cars-smarter.html

http://www.reuters.tv/v/lts/2017/01/08/a-web-of-self-driving-tech-alliances-build-up

Semeoticons, a facial recognition project a project from the Italian National Research Council http://www.semeoticons.eu/?page_id=577

Honda Co-operative Mobility Ecosystem http://www.multivu.com/players/English/7988331-honda-ces-cooperative-mobility-ecosystem/

http://www.ibm.com/cognitive/advantage-reports/

Regulations

http://cyberlaw.stanford.edu/about/people

https://www.washingtonpost.com/local/trafficandcommuting/self-driving-cars-reach-a-fork-in-the-road-and-automakers-take-different-routes/2016/08/24/5cdeaba8-63d9-11e6-8b27-bb8ba39497a2_story.html?utm_term=.a10542879146)

Twizy   http://press.renault.co.uk/press-release/fb984a0e-7b5e-4f09-9c17-02fb185bd49d

REF https://www.youtube.com/watch?v=QXPXK827O0IObject

Personal Mobility

http://www.plugincars.com/honda-unveils-new-personal-people-mover.html

http://www.dailymail.co.uk/sciencetech/article-3902438/The-UFO-ride-work-Ford-engineer-unveils-bizarre-stand-car-concept.html

https://techcrunch.com/2017/04/06/einrides-electric-self-driving-t-pod-is-a-new-kind-of-freight-transport-vehicle/

The IoT Show Archives (http://www.iotdisruptions.com)

IoT Show on YouTube
http://www.youtube.com/c/TheIoTShowbySudhaJamthe

Future of IoT – Devices with Emotions with Prof. Ahmed Banafa
https://www.youtube.com/watch?v=NsJRRVXUjfc

Audi   Brochure   Hack   video   from   The   IoT   Show
https://www.youtube.com/watch?v=EYMCFAjHwRM

IoT and Social – The IoT Show with Guest Ken Herron

https://www.youtube.com/watch?v=ykF5LEx3K1I

Other Books by The Author

Jamthe, Sudha IoT Disruptions 2020: Getting to the Connected World of 2020 with Deep Learning IoT (Futurist guide for entrepreneurs and innovators on how to use Machine Learning/Deep Learning to transform their business to get to 2020)(ISBN-13: 978-1519503411)

Jamthe, Sudha *Internet of Things Business Primer (a case study based book about How to Build an* IoT Business) (ISBN 978-1518800629)

Jamthe, Sudha, *IoT Disruption Kindle book* (good beginners' intro to IoT Landscape)

Jamthe, Sudha, 2030 The Driverless World kindle book (Futuristic view on the Autonomous Vehicle Landscape and Business Disruption)

Epilogue by Rob Van Kranenburg

On Mobility

"Our things in our hands must be equals,"

Aleksandr Rodchenko

Sipping his tea, he looked suddenly up and asked her out of the blue if she had ever read *The Chrysalids* by John Wyndham? She kept looking at her shoes and shook her head. This is how it begins he whispered:

"When I was quite small I would sometimes dream of a city - which was strange because it began before I even knew what a city was. But this city, clustered on the curve of a big blue bay, would come into my mind. I could see the streets, and the buildings that lined them, the waterfront, even boats in the harbour; yet, waking, I had never seen the sea, or a boat. ..."

Once upon a time there was a little boy who was always doing his best, at whatever it was, she could not help thinking and she smiled. And did you know that in WWII the Germans – in an attempt to confuse the Allied pilots – covered large areas with nets or painted wooden structures. And one night one single RAF plane flew over the 'village' and dropped one wooden bomb.

Really? She was interested now. This was a beautiful moment indeed, she could clearly hear the 'thud' as it hit the wooden structure. And why is that such a beautiful story to you?

Well, it shows that there is such a thing as adequate response, a tailored solution to a problem and that people are capable of making rational decisions with a heart and humour. There is a style in an act like that this is taking us all out of our fear of living. I mean do you recall how not so long ago we had cars on petrol and gas even as we knew how bad that was and that it was even a resource that was nearly gone from the earth?

Yes, he said, it is quite unbelievable looking back on those days. It seems like a strange dream. And do you remember how hard it was to change that situation? It seemed as if it would never change, as long as we were in that loop of arguments that all converged in the idea that this was normal.

And also this is quite easy to explain, she sighed. René Thom, the mathematician, says that „each creation and destruction of forms, or morphogenesis, can be described as the disappearance of the attractors that determined the forms that were current, and the replacement of those by capturing of the attractors that represent the eventual forms" (Thom, 1975, cited in Sheldrake, Rupert. The

Rebirth of Nature, 1991)

The forms will not disappear before the attractors that give them their shape have lost their glamour.

So that is what happened. She looked at him and smiled. The car manufacturers lost the success factors that led to the 'car' being their product'. They realized their real offering was not traveling in space but traveling in time.

Listen to Sudha Jamthe's time travel from 2030 to learn how to transform mobility and the disruptions to adapt automotive and transportation industries.

Acknowledgments

I am thankful to my Mom my No.1 cheerleader who makes me feel that the world is limitless, every single day. My daughter Neha Jamthe, you stopped me from tailgating the Google self-driving cars so many times. You are my creative director in translating my time traveler vision onto my book cover. You also contributed the Google self-driving car picture and cover design. I am humbled and blessed to be your Mom.

Thanks to my husband Shirish Jamthe, who has been learning self-driving car at Udacity online and is obsessed with it. As we drive, he has been pointing at lanes and curbs asking, 'How will a self-driving car see this in Computer Vision?'. I saw something else. I saw jaywalking pedestrians and how we wave and nod at people as human drivers. That led me to wonder how the Driverless car needs an AI to understand the nuances of human communication to co-exist with human drivers. I combined that with IoT and came up with futuristic ideas about how traffic lights, road, parking lots, even wearables on our body will become Cognitive IoT and communicate with the car. This will transform businesses, our urban mobility and cities and create innovation opportunities.

That is how this book was born. I am thankful to Shirish's love of machine learning and Driverless car technology and his patience in teaching me the power of machine learning and the many nuances of different algorithms as I tried to see what the car saw on the road.

Sebastian Thurn, Oliver Cameron and the Udacity team, you do not know me. But Sebastian Thrun and Katie Malone's Machine Learning class, Sebastian Thurn's TED talk about the Google self-driving car has fed my curiosity and held my hands and taught me to appreciate the power of data in Cognitive IoT. You have inspired me to bring Driverless car technology and Cognitive IoT together. Thank You.

Oliver Cameron, your tweets sharing every model developed by your self-driving car students gives me hope of an open source software, interoperable technology for the future of driverless cars. Thank You.

Thank You Kyle Columbus of Mercedes benz R&D Center your contagious passion for the autonomous world and for your trust and support for my Stanford CSP Self-Driving cars business course.

The many innovators of the 33 global companies piloting Driverless cars by 2017, your innovation is the seed for this phenomenon. I am thankful that you are doing what you are doing, iterating with each disengagement and building the Driverless world of the future. Thank You.

As always, I aspire to continue this research and engagement with you, my readers and will develop this into a print book. Thank You to so many of my Stanford students and readers for discussions, questions and inspiration about future of tech, IoT and AI. Richard Meyers, requires special mention for his endless curiosity and patience in challenging my thinking about the many paths to the Driverless world.

I am so blessed by the many people who believe in me and cheer me as I embark on each new crazy project. You make me fly, making me believe that the world is limitless.

To Rob Van Kranenburg, Ajit Joakar of Oxford University, Martin Spindler of EU IoT Council who gave me pointers and engaged me through my discovery of Cognitive IoT and the regulations and communications of a Driverless car. Thank You Sally A. Applin and Michael D. Fisher from the University of Kent for your research about multiple communications in Automobiles as pioneers in 2012. Thank You, Ken Herron for seeding the concept of Social IoT and making me understand the need for communications of a Driverless car.

Prof. Rosalind W. Picard of MIT, you don't know me, but your work on Affective computing is my inspiration and hope that we can get the Driverless car to communicate with the human driver with a car AI.

David Newman, thank you for your patience with my never-ending questions about graphics. Natascha Thomson, Petra Ner, Shuchi Rana, thank you, for your moral support on my down days.

Everyone of my readers, students and conference keynote speech followers, who keeps challenging me and keeps me in a learning mode, and sometimes grounding me!

I am nothing without you.

Thank You, Hiru Letap for cheering me with every project and all my writing. Susanna Maier, but for your relentless, endless cycles of editorial feedback this book will not exist. Thank You, Kajal Gupta for getting me to cleanup my web site to the new one http://driverlesscarbook.com. Jeremiah Owyang you don't know how much your pondering questions inspire me to develop futuristic ideas that are grounded in business reality. Waleed Abdulla, your data science camp session on Tensorflow was timely about how car looks at objects.

Marsha Collier and Brian Solis, you are my role models of where I want to be as an author. Thank you.

And to my admin Amy, from x.ai, who is an AI, thank you for keeping me productive.

Thank You Jeff Keni Pulver, for giving me the opportunity to speak about the many conversations of a Driverless car at MoNage conf in San Jose where I have chosen to launch this book (Mar 23rd 2017) for general availability.

To you my reader! You have trusted me and have begun this journey with me. I am here only because of You! Thank You!

About The Author

Sudha Jamthe is the CEO of IoTDisruptions.com and a globally recognized Technology Futurist with 20+ year mix of entrepreneurial, academic and operational experience. Sudha loves shaping new technology ecosystems and mentoring business leaders on digital global transformation strategies.

She is the author of three IoT books, 'IoT Disruption', 'The Internet of Things Business Primer' and 'IoT Disruptions 2020' and one book on Autonomous Vehicles "2030 The Driverless World". Her specialty is business model evolutions and advising business innovators on gaps to innovate. Sudha teaches "How to build a successful Internet of Things Business" course and "The Business of Self-Driving Cars' course at Stanford Continuing Studies Program. She hosts "The IoT Show" on YouTube to bring global practioners interviews in IoT, AI and AV space.

Sudha is a champion for STEM programs and Girls Who Code. Earlier she has served as a venture mentor at MIT and Director of Bay Area Facebook, Twitter, Pinterest and Google+ Meetups. She actively contributes to TechCrunch, Mashable, Venturebeat as a respected technology futurist and blogs on Huffington Post.

She is the chair of the strategic advisory board of Barcelona Technology School, developing digital transformation leaders, member of IEEE global initiative on ethical considerations on the fail-safe development of autonomous and intelligent systems, on the Advisory to Dean College of Engineering, Northwestern Polytechnic University and a proud member of the EU IOT Council.

You can reach her at http:// driverlesscarbook.com or @sujamthe on Twitter.

Praise For Sudha Jamthe's IoT Books

"Sudha Jamthe's no-nonsense approach to IoT is refreshing, informative, and thorough. Read The Internet of Things Business Primer if you want to succeed in the IoT ecosystem." - **Ben Parr, Author of _Captivology_, CEO of Co-founder/CMO Octane AI & one of Inc.'s Top 10 IoT Experts**

Sudha brings case studies from IoT Entrepreneurs and Product Builders globally and combines it with in-depth analysis from her own experience with Mobile Products to offer a must-read book about how to build a successful IoT Business. Watch out this is one of those books you are going to read and re-read many times to serve as your bible as the IoT ecosystem shapes out over the next few years."- **Myles Weissleder SF NewTech Meetup Founder**

"The Internet of Things Business Primer" is a guidebook for innovators, entrepreneurs and technology leaders looking for practical examples of best practices to build a successful IoT business. Sudha brings her own experience and the one of other entrepreneurs that have had a meaningful impact on charting the path of the IoT industry" - **Davide Vigano, CEO Sensoria Inc.**

"Analysis of IoT from a business perspective by a seasoned business and product leader – that is what this book is all about. Sudha has done an amazing job in evaluating IoT and has shown us how to make a business out of it. This is not an easy task and Sudha has done complete justice to it." - **Pragati Rai Sr Innovation specialist Deutsche Bank & Author Android Application Security Essentials**

"Sudha is an amazing thought leader in the new and exciting field of IoT. She is talented and inspiring with her words and work. Its exciting to see her put her deep knowledge of IoT and sharp vision of the future of this trend of technology into this book" - **Ahmed Banafa, Professor San Jose State University**

" We live in a connected world that continues to evolve each day. And therein lies the opportunity to build a business. Sudha Jamthe brings her years of experience as a technologist to this comprehensive guide, applying her own experience, and drawing from others in case studies that solidify important concepts. *The Internet of Things Business Primer* is a the definitive source for anyone looking to blaze a path in the IoT world and be successful doing it." - **Frank Gruber CEO and Cofounder of Tech.co and**

Author Startup Mixology

"Sudha Jamthe's new book provides the definitive roadmap for building an IoT business and navigating the forthcoming disruption across many industries with a comprehensive overview covering technology, business models and use cases" - **Ajit Jaokar Author of Data Science for IoT and CEO Futuretext.**

"I really enjoyed Sudha's first book "IoT Disruptions" that covers the universe of opportunities that IoT is bringing to our lives. This book "The Internet of Things Business Primer" goes deeper to offer an in-depth guide and case studies for anyone who wants to learn how to build an IoT Business to accelerate the digital transformation."- **Josep Clotet, Founding Managing Director, Barcelona Technology School**

"Sudha is a great supporter of the grassroots of Silicon Valley. I had the honor to work with her, when developing Startup Weekend back in 2010 with eBay and PayPal. In this book Sudha is leveraging her unique insight to prepare the next wave of innovation and support the IoT community. This is not another book about IoT, this is a map on how to navigate the future of IoT entrepreneurship." - **Franck Nouyrigat. Co-founder Global Startup Weekend and Partner recorp**

'I have known Sudha for many years and she is highly respected for her insights in developing products for the 21st century. She really is a visionary, able to spot new technology trends in the social and mobile arenas. Read this book, slowly and digest her advice. I suspect you will refer back to it many times' - **Brian Solis, Principal Analyst, Altimeter Group, a Prophet company.**

Made in the USA
San Bernardino, CA
06 November 2019